KARATE
Beginner to Black Belt

KARATE
Beginner to Black Belt

by

H. D. PLÉE

5th Dan Karate, 4th Dan Judo, 2nd Dan Aikido
Technical Director of the Karate Section of the
French Federation of Judo and Associated Disciplines
Secretary of the European Karate Union

Translated and Edited by
Iain Morris, 2nd Dan Judo

LONDON
W. FOULSHAM & CO. LTD.
NEW YORK · TORONTO · CAPE TOWN · SYDNEY

W. FOULSHAM & CO. LTD.
Yeovil Road, Slough, Berks., England

ISBN 0-572-00086-3

Printed in Great Britain by
St Edmundsbury Press, Bury St Edmunds, Suffolk

H. D. PLÉE

5th Dan Japanese KARATE
4th Dan JUDO
2nd Dan AIKIDO
Honorary President of the
French Federation of Judo and
Associated Disciplines.
President of the Karate
Technical Commission.

I dedicate this book
        to my son
        to my pupils
        to my friends and teachers
        Ohshima, Harada, Tani, Yamaguchi, Ogasahara,
        Hironishi, Oyama, Nishiyama, Mochizuki,
who voluntarily, or involuntarily allowed me to write it for you.

CONTENTS

PREFACE

The latest among the sports of combat and defence to put in an appearance, KARATE has caught up on its late start with giant strides and now surpasses its elders in many respects.

It has even taken the place of Ju-Jitsu and Judo in that part of the public mind which is interested in the strange and wonderful, and when children, or the writers of sensational novels and films want to speak of decisive attack or counter-attack, they speak of KARATE.

In this book, I have described KARATE as if explaining it to my friends over tea. While avoiding monotony, I have tried at the same time to convey important advice and to be as clear as possible, so that you will have the true outline of KARATE: a magnificent, absorbing ART; a virile, exciting sport; a complete, incontestable DEFENCE; a MASTERY of body and spirit which will lead to a widening of the whole personality.

This is not the first work on the subject of KARATE, but I am conscious of having released the essentials of true Karate in order that the reader, of whatever school, may rediscover the "way". All styles (expressions of different levels and values) are reunited in the higher grades.

The practising beginner will find all that he needs to know in order to attain a Black Belt. Other books would no doubt be useful to him, but if he has but this one, he will possess all the indispensable bases.

I am aware of the difficulty of my task; much of what I tell is being revealed for the first time. Even in JAPAN, certain of the advice which follows is transmitted by word of mouth only. This assertion is not just publicity, but a simple statement of fact. In addition, I am not certain that their deeper meaning will be immediately understood. Certain passages, while apparently very simple, can be understood only in proportion to the degree of advancement. My hope is that the reader of these lines will be captivated by KARATE, and that he will become an enthusiastic Black Belt as well . . . soon.

With friendly greetings,
from the French Academy of Martial Arts.
34 rue Montagne-Sainte-Genevieve, PARIS V.

Master FUNAKOSHI Gichin

Introduction to Karate

Some people think when they enter Karate that the Sensei (Professor of Martial Arts) under whom they place themselves, will give them a superior power, the secrets of strength, new holds or techniques, which will enable them after a short time to beat anyone and to become a sort of "superman".

I must tell you honestly that I can "give" you nothing. If this were possible, be assured that I would do so immediately. All that a teacher can do is to point the way to those who really want to make progress, and eventually, to draw out the real strength that is in you, and to reveal you to yourself. For this "superman" power is in you all without exception. Even women

10

and children. It is pent up, preserved and enveloped by your conscious and subconscious mind, your habits, customs and education. The object of Karate is to release this virile human power, this life in you, and make it perform its natural functions. Sometimes, this can be very hard, even cruel, and you may find yourself hating the "Old Man" or the "Sensei" who has imposed such a severe test on you . . . but you will be transformed.

In order to cut through these psychic blocks, complexes and harmful reflexes, you should think of them as like the many fine layers of thought and habit which by hard training you can peel away one by one like the layers of an onion, until, suddenly, you reach the heart. It is therefore necessary at every training period not merely to repeat the movements, but to seek to push yourself beyond the limits of your concentration, perception, speed and resistance, according to the circumstances.

In this manual for beginners, which will probably be very useful also to those who have been graded, I have tried to transmit the spirit and the feeling of true Karate, rather than the beauty of its external form. If you strive from the outset to bring forth the true power of your body, heart and spirit, the beauty will follow as a matter of course. But not the reverse.

I have proved that the Dojos and the styles which attach too much importance to appearances make but slow and limited progress. Only sincerity of movement and a continual desire for self-perfection will bring rewards.

When I became the pioneer of European Karate in 1948, nobody had heard of the word Karate. Some people even thought that it was a pure invention on my part, and called it "Karaplee". Over a period of ten years, with no genuine expert to guide me, I engaged in the excitement of combat because this was my temperament in Judo. My style was very imperfect when compared with films and photographs from Japan, but I was indifferent to grades; my sole concern was the mental and physical enrichment brought about by Karate. After that, I sent for five successive Karateka from Japan at my own expense, and my style improved rapidly because I practised with enthusiasm. When I had been to China and then to Japan in order to study the modern styles and perfect my own ability, I had the surprise to be nominated 5th Dan (the highest grade in Karate). The Japanese teachers considered—to my embarrassment— that I had mastered the true Karate up to a level beyond which nobody can honestly judge (intuitive, mental, etc.) for there are no longer any limits. I believe that this example shows the importance of practising thoroughly and honestly, without dreaming of quick success or of grades. The reward will then come when you least expect it. This is the best short cut of all.

Nobody can attain complete mastery, that is to say, 100 per cent of his mental, physical and spiritual capabilities. Perfection is not of this world, or it is reserved for very few human beings. Therefore it is necessary to continue to practise throughout your life (according to age and capability) and to try to approach the truth about yourself. And this whatever the age, state of health, or family or social status.

I receive so many letters from people studying on their own, and who despair of finding practical advice and instruction in popular Karate books. These are the people I have thought of above all when writing this book. One cannot perform really great Karate alone, but one can enter deeply into the feelings as I did myself when I started. With the aid of this book, by reading everything written about Karate, by films and slides, one can reach as high as black-belt level. Sometimes, further than those who go to a Dojo and wait for the Professor to give them everything, without effort. But it requires much courage and perseverance.

It must be understood that the different works are necessary according to the practitioner's level, for Karate has very differing aspects depending on the stage of progress reached: the purely technical evolution (the positioning of the feet, the orientation of the trunk, etc.) or the mental (offensive, defensive, non-mental, intuitive, etc.).   This is too big a subject to be developed here, but it must be said that many Karate men stagnate because of their ignorance of this progression.

It is very easy to perform an imitation Karate, and this is what many people do. Their actions are fast and attractive, as are their Katas; their resolution also leaves little to be desired. But it is empty inside. They avoid competition and are never put to the test. This is a great pity, for it cannot but accentuate their complexes and faults. To perform true Karate demands hard, honest work over a period of at least five years (as in all other fields) and generally for a lifetime.

If you succeed in grasping the fundamental principles and advice contained in this book, the remaining Karate techniques and also those of other combat sports, will seem easy to you. I wrote, at the same time as "Karate—Beginner to Black Belt", other more advanced books in which I developed all the advice contained—sometimes very briefly—in the following pages. And in which I described the Katas in more profound detail, including some very important ones, such as the Ten-no-Kata (Heavenly Kata) which the Master Funakoshi considered to be the beginning and end of Karate. At the age of 88, he practised every day. A week before he died he still practised, seated on the edge of his bed, and he said, "I believe that I am beginning to feel the true tsuki". This brought tears to the eyes of his pupils, and they thought, "the Master is dying, never before has he claimed to be attaining mastery". It is to this humble spirit and this resolute decision to be continually seeking self-improvement that you should turn your thoughts when looking at the photograph of the old Master on page 10.

Good points: Intent regard, hips strong.
Fault: Lack of stability in the leg (heel raised).

Numerous faults due to lack of concentration and stability (heel raised).

What is Karate?

With fencing, Karate is probably the oldest MARTIAL ART, that is to say, the oldest fighting technique of killing and avoiding being killed. For Judo, the creation of Dr. Jigoro Kano, dates back 80 years (1882); Ju-Jitsu dates back 250 years (the Kodokan archives show the first signs of its existence in 1648); Karate goes back to the earliest written records on earth, the Chinese texts of some 3,000 years ago. They tell of this "technique intended to maintain the body and spirit in condition solely through teaching the means of fighting with arms or without arms". (The movements are the same whether bare-handed or using side arms).

"Empty Hand" or "Chinese Boxing" are the translations of the names generally used in China or the other countries of the East where this technique is practised. For our part, we shall use the Japanese term Karate, which means "empty hand", to describe the techniques of fighting with the body's natural weapons.

But there is a risk that the number of different schools of training and conceptions of fighting may sow seeds of confusion in ill-informed minds. This is particularly the case in America, where there are nine different Japanese styles (out of the 15 styles in Japan), three Chinese, two Korean and two Okinawan styles, resulting from emigration and the Eastern wars.

We have passed the period of hostility from Judo. Seeing that the growing popularity of Karate has not involved any diminution in the number of Judo players (Judo is a marvellously well-balanced sport), they have generally left the "self-defence" branch to Karate, for in this field the efficacy of Karate has become, and is recognised as being, incontestable.

One must not lose sight of the fact that Karate is "all-in" fighting. Everything is allowed: every effective method in no matter what other form of combat sport exists in Karate, re-directed under the dramatic conditions of a man's desperate fight for life, using the means given to him by nature. This is why Karate is based on blows delivered with the hand, the foot, the head or the knee. Equally permissible are strangulations, throwing techniques, locks (though certain typically Karate methods are unusable in either boxing or Judo). This is one of the fascinating things about taking up Karate; this sensation of mastery over all the effective techniques brings an inner peace and calm which is difficult to find in combat sports using arms, or in those which contain the limitations and restrictions of a sporting objective.

The only forbidden act in Karate is to injure a training partner or a competition opponent. Avoiding this demands great skill. Also, part of the training is centred around exercises performed in space or against an imaginary opponent (as in shadow-boxing) during which one attacks without reserve, and with the genuine feeling that the purpose is "to kill in order not to be killed". This training can be continued to an advanced age, modified, of course, in its rhythm and expression.

It is my wish that this book will enlighten you about an art that is still regarded as a little mysterious in the West, and one in which it can be said that I have attained a certain mastery.

One cannot claim that one style is superior to another. The fight for life must be adapted according to the build of the one who is defending and to the one who is attacking, depending on the circumstances. All techniques are valid in theory. In practice, real efficacy is an attribute only of those techniques which are well known.

Origins

Born in India, where it was invented by the religious in order to counter the harmful effects of prolonged meditation and, it is said, to enable the monks to defend themselves without arms against the numerous bandits of that period, Karate (for that is the term which we shall use henceforth to describe all styles, even the Chinese) spread throughout Southern China, then the North, and eventually to all the Chinese colonies in Asia. Among these, Okinawa became the real cradle of the violent and effective Karate style of modern Japan, while the other Asiatic styles relapsed into mental pursuits and consequently lost more or less of their violent objective.

It seems that the first transformation of Karate as a source of physical well-being into Martial Karate, took place in the armies of Alexander the Great. Having invaded India without major difficulties, Alexander authorised his resting troops to keep themselves occupied by means of tournaments in which they fought all-in and without arms. These proved a tremendous success.

The study of Karate, once practised by the monks in secret, now became transformed, and was used in the course of encounters which greatly appealed to the population. The popular diffusion of Karate throughout China and Asia dates from this period.

Every region practised it in a slightly different way. For instance, the Chinese of the South, people of the fishing boats and swampy rice fields, made great use of the upper part of the body without moving or using—or very little—their lower limbs, while the Chinese of the North, who were huntsmen, insisted on the importance of attacks with the feet, together with the jumps and acrobatics which are still used in the Chinese Theatre.

Faults: Bad judgement of distance
and lack of physical concentration.

One can appreciate already by means of these two brief examples the differences which could appear within the regions; but in every region, the styles themselves also differed according to the Professors and their physical properties. Thickset men preferred direct blocks, small changes in bodily position and strong attacks. Slim men preferred flexible defences, evasions, supple changes of position, and long-range striking attacks. If one adds the fact that in the imitation of fighting birds and animals (tigers, monkeys, eagles, herons, horses, etc.) also influenced the styles, and even certain stratagems (such as imitating a drunken man), one has a better understanding of the great diversity of forms.

MacArthur Decides

We no longer have the credulity of the Middle Ages, when the natural ability of one man could bring a whole school in its train, full of astonishing theories, naïvety and error.

Through other sports, through scientific laws (the law of Newton, the conditioned reflexes of Pavlov, etc. . . .) we can distinguish the effective principles and the valid techniques—without finding it necessary to kill the guinea-pigs or to risk our lives in bare-handed duels, as in the past.

On the right, a good commencement for Tobi-Tsuki.

In the course of World Championships and the Olympic Games, one can confirm that the best men, the Champions, use techniques in their particular disciplines which are very close, if not strictly alike. And that, in spite of the fact that there are several schools, such as the French, Hungarian and Italian in fencing.

Logic tells us that there can be only one really effective style for the best use of our energy, to attack and to parry. And this is the case in Karate.

I have my own personal opinions, of course, but as I do not wish to become involved in partisan feuds, I shall merely say that there are three large, genuine schools (SHOTOKAN, SHITO-RYU, GOJU-RYU) which have given rise to numerous other schools of a generally inferior quality. The majority of these "deviationists" are the post-war schools, born from the immense popularity of Karate which, alone, was permitted by General MacArthur ("Chinese Boxing", as well as Judo, Kendo and Aikido, were banned). Financial conditions were hard. It was necessary for the Karate men of average ability to show originality in order to attract pupils. Karate Championships, an innovation both happy and unhappy at the same time, led to a real revolution against tradition. It presented a new aspect and caused many to abandon the idea of an all-in fight to the death against several opponents, and to concentrate their training on competition against a single adversary. This was the case in many universities, and in several schools such as the WADO-RYU and the SHUKOKAI, now well known in the West thanks to their enthusiastic representatives.

For my part, according to my experience and my comparative studies in Japan, I am certain that a synthesis can be made from the basic schools. Particularly on the basis of the Shotokan; this is what I have done for my own pupils, and for eight years they have carried off all the titles and practised the Katas of all schools.

Perhaps one can find in the desire of so many Karate men to form a strong attachment to a particular school, the fact that there are so few works on Karate. I mean by this, works giving the practical bases, and not those giving general descriptions with no detailed instructions for putting them into effect.

———————————

It is easy to teach the superficialities of Karate; it is more difficult to transmit its real efficacy, and its mental possibilities. This requires a deep knowledge, experience and a natural gift for teaching.

18

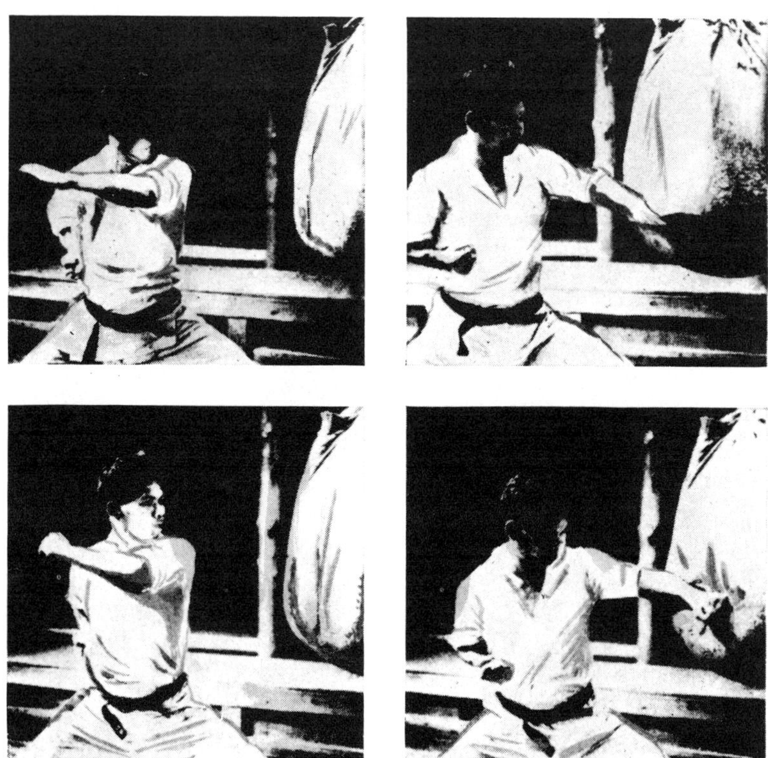

Master Funakoshi's son Yoshitaka Funakoshi, the greatest genius in the history of Karate, who died of starvation during the occupation after refusing American rations.

Baroux, Champion of Europe 1966 and 1967

The Karate of Okinawa

Very skilful at assimilating the discoveries of others, the Japanese frequently give these discoveries new orientations which lead to considerable progress. Perhaps because they see them through new eyes. This was the case with Japanese Karate, which was born in Okinawa but never really asserted itself until it reached Japan.

Okinawa practised Chinese Karate as did the other countries of Asia, that is to say, as an art filled with poetry, slow movements, non-violence and mental concentration. Then suddenly, the possession of arms in the island was declared a crime against the Chinese state. The inhabitants immediately searched for means of transforming their art into a technique aimed at killing their oppressors. This was the origin of the hardening techniques using the Makiwara (a post covered with interwoven straw) and the fast, strong and ruthless attacking movements. Time passed, and Karate changed again to become what one might almost call a Karate of peace, and of health.

When the Japanese invaded in their turn, they re-introduced the ban on all arms, even the iron batons. Okinawan Karate, or TODE, which means "Chinese Boxing", was transformed anew, but this time to a perfecting of the violent form which lasted until our own days.

The Archives of Napoleon's aide-de-camp indicate that the Emperor exiled on the Isle of Elba was astounded by this prohibition (the isle was invaded in the same epoch, still the Middle Ages in Japan, with firearms practically unknown). He said: "How could they do it without even a baton?", and he sent a mission to investigate.

And of Japan

It is understandable that the Karate Masters of Okinawa would preserve their one weapon against the Japanese invaders for a long time. In fact, it was not until 1917 that a Japanese expert, the Master Funakoshi, agreed to perform the first demonstration in Tokyo. He then returned to Okinawa, refusing to teach. But the demonstration had proved enormously successful. In 1922, the Minister of Sport insisted that the Master return and stage another demonstration, in the course of which he met the Masters Kano (Judo) and Uyeshiba (Aiki). The enthusiasm was such that, having refused his return *visa* to Okinawa, Funakoshi agreed to teach Karate in the universities. This was the first appearance of the basic, fast and light Shutokan style.

Eight years afterwards, seeing Funakoshi's success, his friend Mabuni left Okinawa and settled in the Kyoto region where he created the Shitoryu style. This was similar in conception and was, in fact, the same school, but Mabuni had previously studied the rather more elevated and powerful Go-Ju style.

Then, the Master Miyagi displayed and taught the Gojuryu style, the traditional and most ancient form in Okinawa, where the researches into strength went very deep, and which was characterised by small movements of the body and sonorous respiration. All the other styles derived from these three schools, with occasional Chinese contributions, or certain personal characteristics and faults of the Professors.

Training in the Dojo

It is rarely that one can get within a hundred yards of a Karate Dojo without hearing the cries (Kiai), which are listened to by the neighbours with a mixture of resignation and respect.

When one enters the DOJO the atmosphere is often different to that which one expects. According to the training in progress, the couples attack each other fiercely, jump, dodge, and counter-attack on the polished parquet (if the DOJO is used also for Aiki or Judo, one can sometimes practice on tatami). One can also go into a Kihon course, and then it is an astonishing sight to see the small regiment of men in white kimonos, lined up in four or five rows, advancing step by step as they strike or parry imaginary blows and again uttering the loud shouts designed to bring forth the bodily energy. One experiences the curious sensation of a rising tide, impossible to dam. But if one enters the dojo while the Katas are in progress, the feeling of strangeness is complete, for they do not resemble any Western exercises. The Karateka are arranged in equal rows, and at the orders of the Sensei (title of the Professor) they defend, attack, turn, cry out, all at the same time, in apparently complicated patterns, and one really has the impression of taking part in a war dance (this is what a Kata is, in effect). In general, the spectators do not smile and they regard this dance attentively, because they can sense the strength and impressive sincerity. The Katas form one of the criteria for attaining Black Belt (it is necessary to know from five to eight for first Dan).

The "Dojo" is the place (Jo) where one seeks the way (Do) to personal mastery throughout the Martial Arts, as others seek the same unity of body and spirit through meditation and mortification (monks, etc. . . . .). It is neither a sports arena nor a gymnasium, neither is it a Temple or a Church, but it is all of these at the same time.

22

Group performance of Eian Shodan in a Dojo

Group performance of Eian Godan in a Dojo.

A course of Karate is strictly conducted. No practitioner is left to train alone during the lessons (unless he is a "senior", in which case he will help and correct the "juniors"). The collective atmosphere (Ki) is essential to the process of surpassing one's own limitations.

After the kneeling bow towards the place of honour (Kamiza), the course begins with suppling movements (Jun-bin-Taisho), then complementary exercises for agility, the muscles and for building up resistance, and a return to calm with special breathing.

Certain schools seek after an extreme simplicity in their training (few technical studies, one very simple Kata), but they push the study of difficulty and the limits of endurance to great lengths. Others, with opposing aims, seek after variety, fanciful studies and the applications to personal defence (this pleases many pupils, but they make little progress). The most reasonable course for beginners under first Dan must certainly lie somewhere between these two.

Before you start, visit several Dojos. If you have the opportunity, try a few training sessions so that you can see which appears to be the better qualified to teach you. Your whole future in Karate, and even your everyday behaviour, depends on this. It is an alarming thought, when one considers that very few non-Japanese instructors are of even average ability, and that many of the Japanese instructors are not psychologically suited to teaching Westerners.

Fortunately, there are Professors who have the ability to take you a long way, but the number is small.

Read as much as you can. If you have the means, buy films. You must love Karate with passion and immerse yourself in it with delight. Make sacrifices. Keep a note book for your observations. Without a whole-hearted involvement you will gain nothing.

Mr. Suzuki, representative of Wado Ryu in Europe.

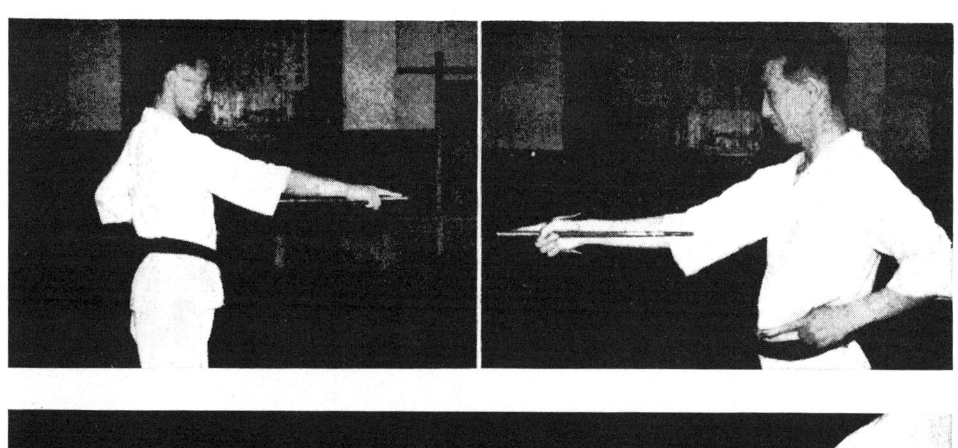

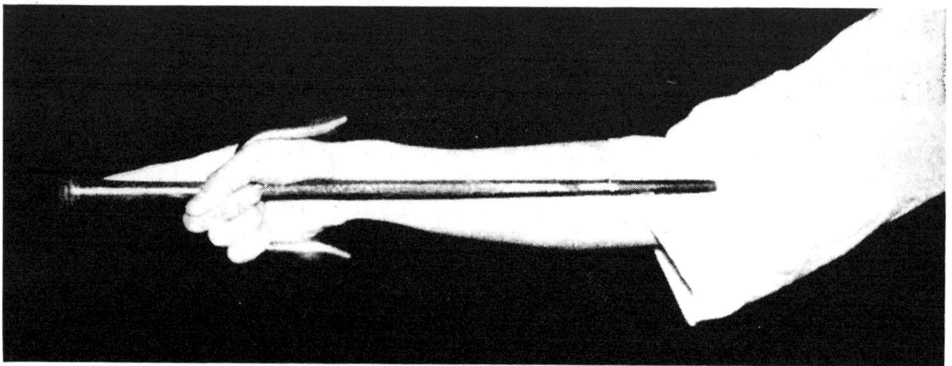

The Sai, an ancient weapon from Okinawa known to all high grade Karateka—it is easy to defend oneself effectively against a man armed with a sword, and to counter-attack with deadly effect—All the katas can be performed with the Sai.

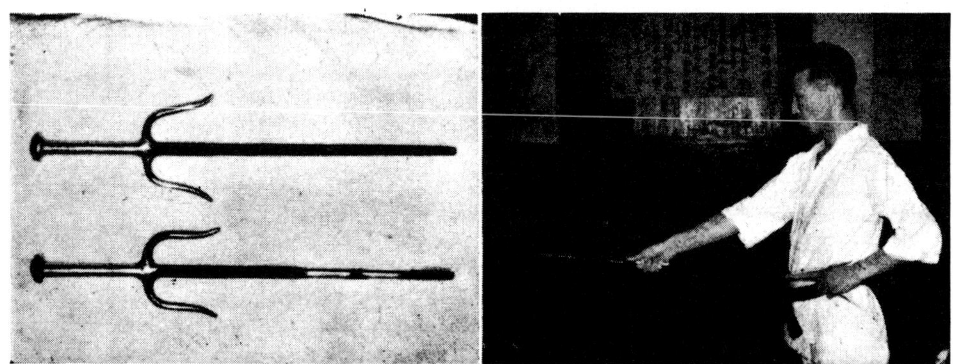

Left:
Shuto
(Edge of the Hand)

Right:
Enpi
(Vertical Elbow)

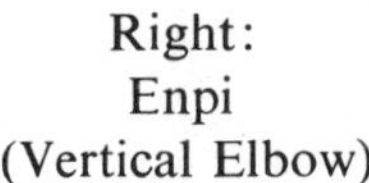
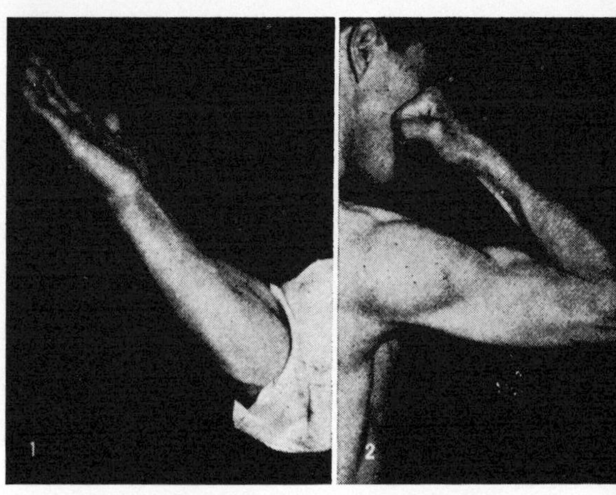

Our Natural Weapons

Our body possesses many natural weapons which can be used with great effect to put an adversary out of action, even one who is armed.

As a protection against certain weapons in times of war, it was sometimes necessary to use a minor article, such as a glove covered with metal plates or points of iron (against a sabre or a knife), or a piece of metal or hard wood to protect the foot, the forearm, or to reinforce the elbow.

For the most part, our own natural weapons can perform the same functions in normal cases. It is, of course, necessary to prepare and accustom them to this use, to strengthen muscles, tendons and bones, and to develop protective pads of fibrous tissue which will enable them to strike with impunity, even against a wall of cement.

Certain natural weapons are well known, such as the basic use of the fist (Seiken), the elbow, used vertically or horizontally (Enpi, Fig. 4 and 5). But there are others, less well known, which can also be very effective, such as the palm (Teisho, Fig. 3), the edge of the hand (Shuto, Fig. 1 and 5), the back of the hand (Haishu, Fig. 5), the heel of the thumb (Haito, the upper part of Haishu, Fig. 5), the finger-tips (Yon-hon-Nukite, Fig. 6), the back of the fist (Uraken or Riken), the side of the fist (Tettsui or "iron hammer"), etc.

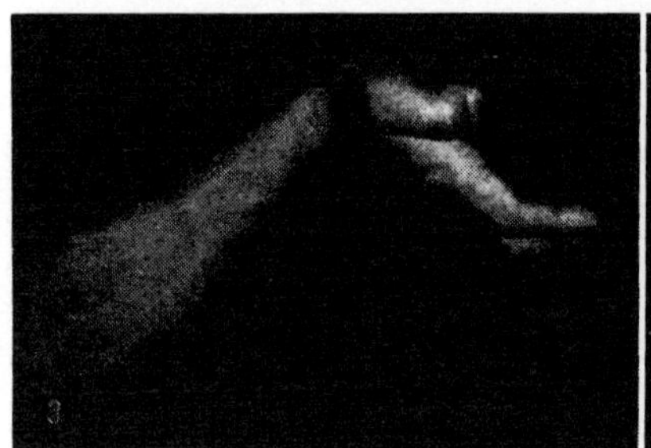

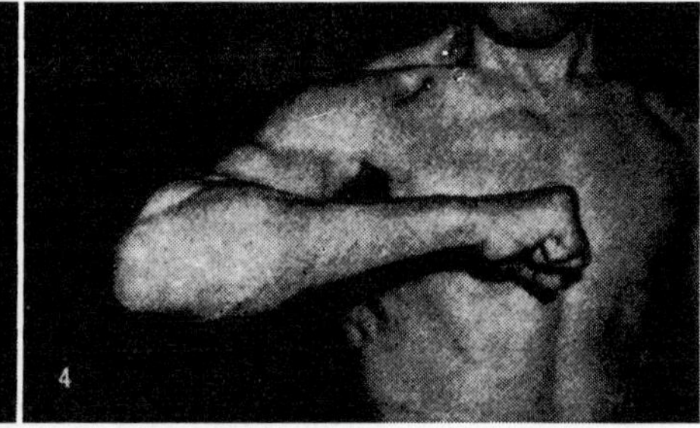

Teisho (Palm)

Enpi (Horizontal Elbow)
Nukite (Finger-tips) and

Shuto (Edge of the Hand)

Haishu (Back of the Hand)

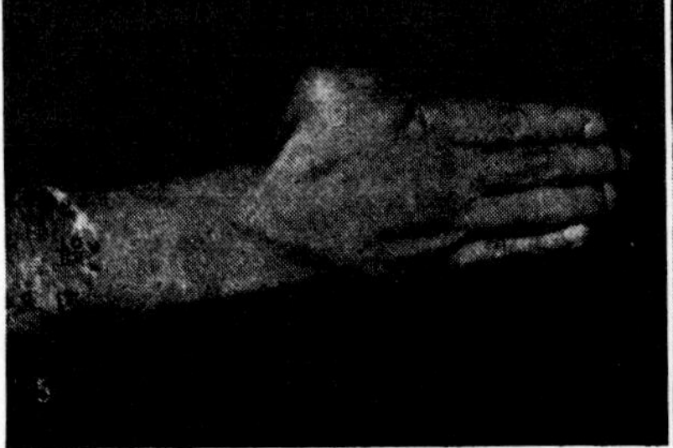

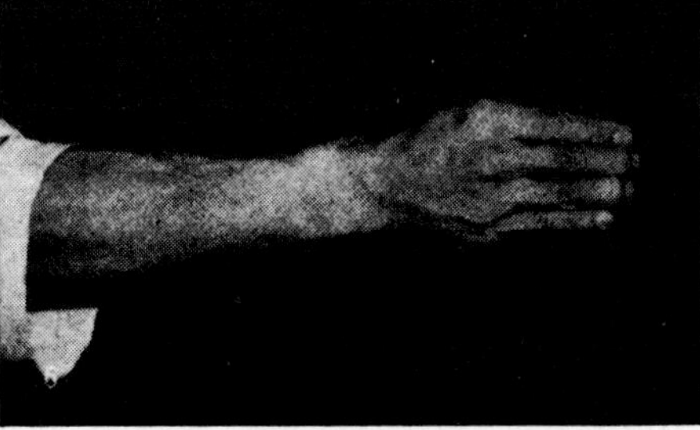

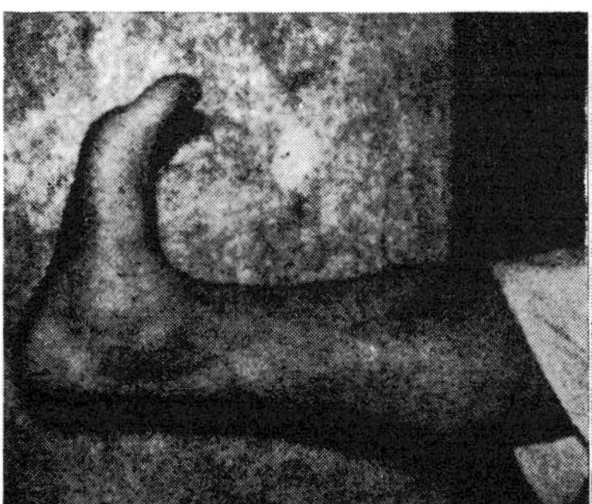

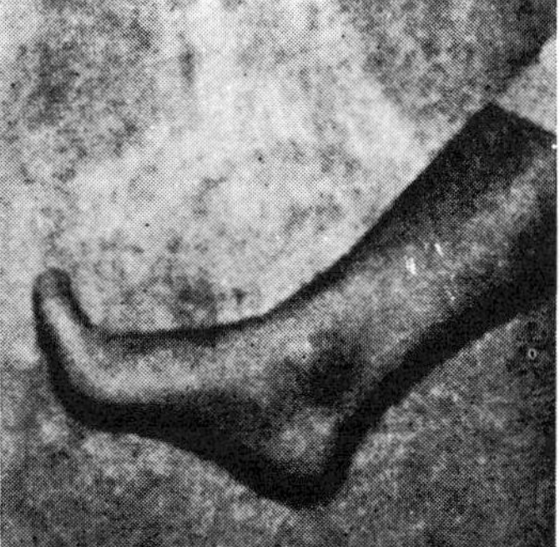

Kagato (Heel)   Koshi (Ball of the Foot)

Power of the Atemi Blow

A mistake with serious consequences has been committed in Japan through the demonstrations and propaganda aimed at popularizing Karate. It is this: by practice and by certain hardening methods, one acquires eventually in Karate a striking force of terrifying power. One can break any bone with the hand, drive the bare fist through a door, smash ten roofing tiles one on top of the other with the edge of the hand, or 16 tiles with the elbow, etc. . . . By stressing this aspect of Karate, the Masters, with the best intentions, have given an erroneous impression of their art. Now, moreover, many Japanese have been persuaded that the Karateka can crush a skull with a blow of his fist, or pierce the thoracic cage or the throat with his fingers and wrench out a vital organ! It is useless to tell of the pains taken by the Karatekas and Master Funakoshi to bring the legends back to reality and to show Karate in its true aspect: a fencing with the limbs and the spirit for the attainment of a total mastery.

Where does this striking power come from? From a training which, as we have said, is rather special, but one with which these exploits can be equalled by anybody. And also by means of a principle according to which "the more the force of the blow is concentrated, the more powerful the impact", proportionate, of course, to the degree of force. Let us take an example:

Let us consider a clenched, gloved fist: the striking surface measures about 10cm. × 5cm., that is, a total of 50cm². Now let us consider Kento, that is to say, the knuckles of the index and middle fingers when the fist is closed (Seiken or better a single ball). Atemi uses these two knuckles only, the total surface area does not exceed 2cm. × 2cm., 25 times less in area and consequently 25 times the power. One obtains the same difference with the edge of the hand, or the finger-tips, among others. You can now understand how the Karateka can realise these "incredible" exploits when his life is in danger. It is limited only by the strength of his own bone structure and his degree of hardness, which is something he learns to recognise by practice. One does not strike in the same way when practising, nor with the same parts, against the strong bones (cranium), the mobile bones (the limbs, jawbone), or the soft parts (sometimes protected by clothes).

Sokuto (Edge of the Foot)

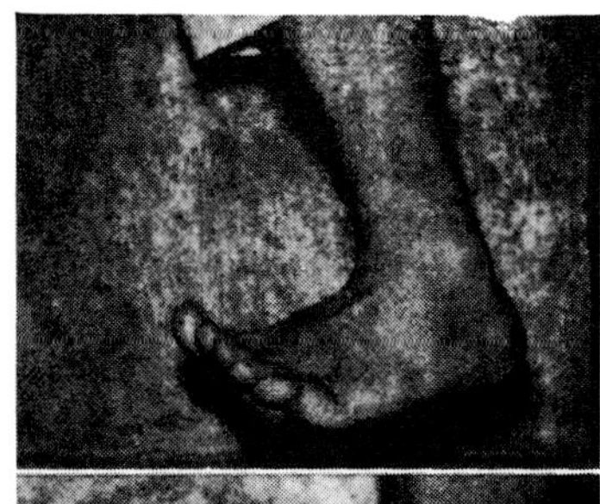

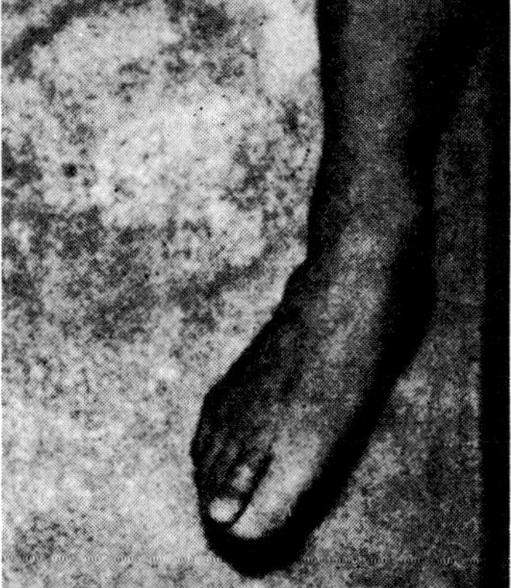

Haisoku (Instep) and Ashinukito (Toes)

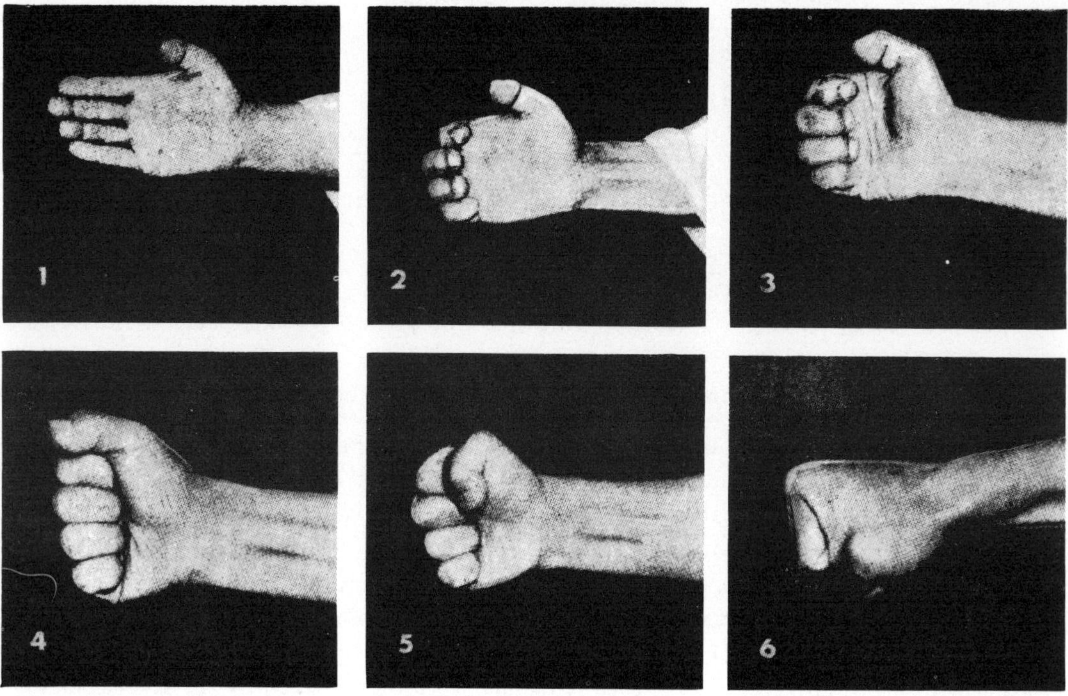

One of the peculiarities of Karate is the use of the feet to ward off an opponent, to turn him aside, to strike and to sweep. Our lower limbs, frequently neglected, are three times stronger than our upper limbs and allow us to reach an opponent from unexpectedly great distances if the technique is correct. One can affirm that a Karateka is never surprised by an ordinary kick in serious combat.

Training in the Dojo is performed with bare feet; this ensures that one is never caught in a position of disadvantage (on the beach, for example). After a few months of exercises one experiences an astonishing sensation of "walking on velvet", proof that the muscles of the lower limbs are being developed and in particular, that the feet, atrophied by the continual wearing of shoes, are being re-educated.

One strikes with the feet according to the same principle as that which applies to the fist, that is to say, one concentrates the force in the smallest possible area of the foot (heel, ball of the foot, the toes themselves).

How to Clench the Fist
It is important to clench the fist correctly (Seiken). Boxers are usually afraid of hitting with the bare fist, not because they punch too hard for the bones of the hand, but because wearing a boxing glove induces certain habits which prevent the hand being clenched correctly. They cannot strike with all their energy any more for fear of bruising the hand.

One does not learn how to clench the fist properly after just a few lessons. It takes many months to achieve. The important thing is not to leave any spaces in the fist and to arrange the fingers so that the hand forms a solid block. Moreover, the position of the wrist permits the per-

28

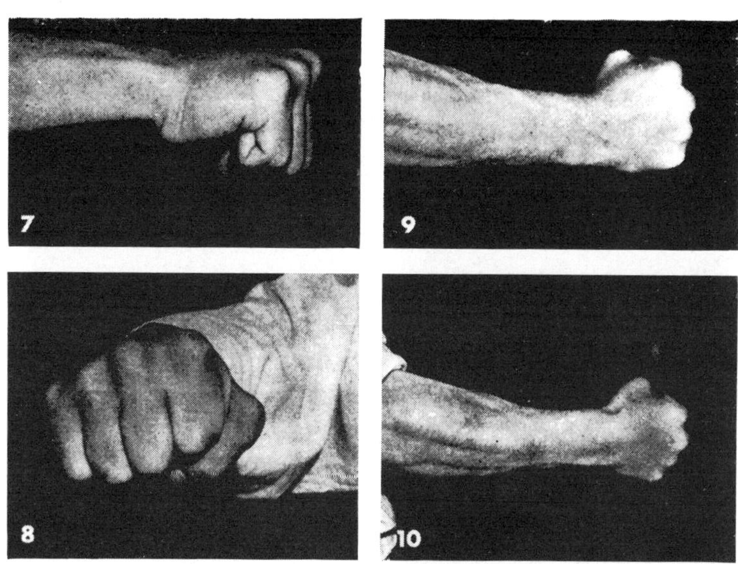

One commences by folding the little finger, then the other fingers which are then locked into position by the thumb. The full force is not put into the fist until the moment of impact, but care must be taken to avoid opening the fist in the course of the attack or to let the little finger relax.

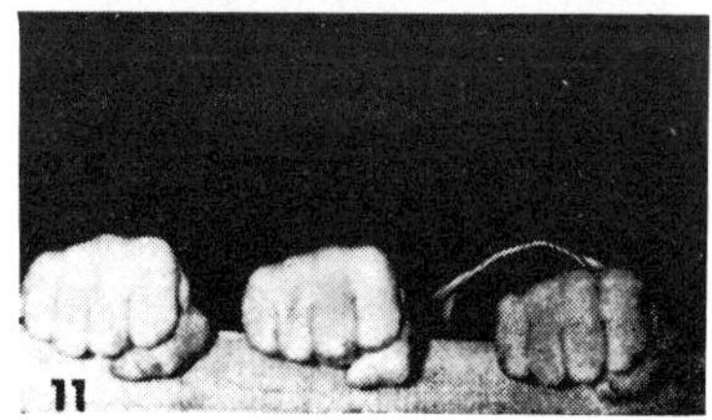

formance of certain almost unbelievable exploits or else causes a fracture, depending on whether it is good or bad. Besides this, time alone can strengthen the bones of the hand by regular training on the Makiwara (post covered with straw).

The back of the fist should be in line with the forearm (Figs. 6 and 7). One strikes with the knuckles of the index and middle fingers (Kento).

The two knuckles must be perfectly in line with the forearm (as in Fig. 10). A strong, direct punch given in the position of Fig. 9 would result in a fracture.

Very often, the most difficult thing to do is to fold the index finger as in Fig. 4. One succeeds after a more or less lengthy training on the Makiwara. All other ways of clenching the fist are dangerous.

By training on the Makiwara, the two knuckles increase in size and permit one to strike with the bases of the index and middle fingers only, or better still, with just the base of the index finger. The first three months (adults) or six months (juniors) can be a bit painful, but this must not be taken seriously. If the skin becomes broken by an excess of zeal in the early stages, the practice should be suspended during the time necessary for scar tissue to form, by persisting one misses carrying out a valuable training.

Never practise blows with the feet on the Makiwara, which is intended for the fist only. For the feet, it is necessary to have a larger and harder Makiwara, or better still, a long, suspended bag of at least 200lb. in weight.

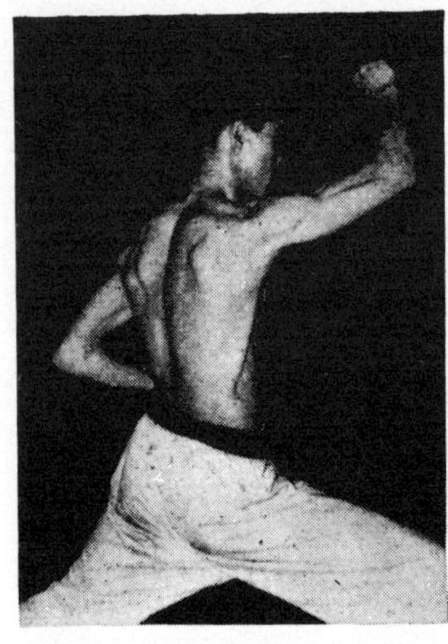

Good
(concentration
of strength)

Bad
(has only the
appearance of
correctness.)

The Concentration of Force

The illustration above shows the method of TSUKI, that is, a direct blow as if plunging in a knife. It seems a little strange to some people, especially those who have already practised a combat sport such as boxing. It is, nevertheless, the most devastating way of hitting. It is the only one which permits the full power of the body to be used in attack. For example, it is the only one which is capable of breaking the rib-cage. In one sense, it has something in common with the "straight" punch in English boxing, but the Tsuki attack is much more interesting from our point of view because it utilizes the whole body without the balance suffering in consequence.

In the photograph on the bottom of the next page, a Japanese expert shows the correct method of hitting with concentration of the muscular force. The photograph at the bottom of this page, on the other hand, looks correct but is in fact wrong. You will probably not be able to see any difference at all, but, little by little, and with practice, you will grasp the full importance.

Look closely. The right shoulder is slightly lower and full of power. The armpit is fully contracted. In this way, it is possible to articulate the right arm or to lock it so firmly with the torso that your attack cannot possibly be deflected. One can attack with the whole body, from the toes right through to the fist. The entire force of the body is directed against the opponent and becomes effective. By repeating this movement many times during every training session,

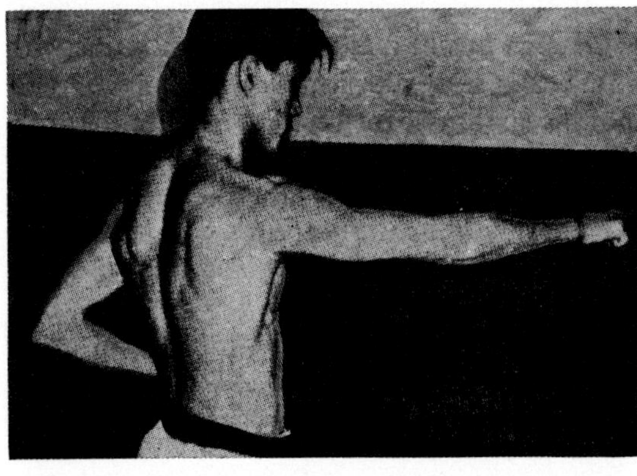

Bad
(no concentration of
strength under the arm)

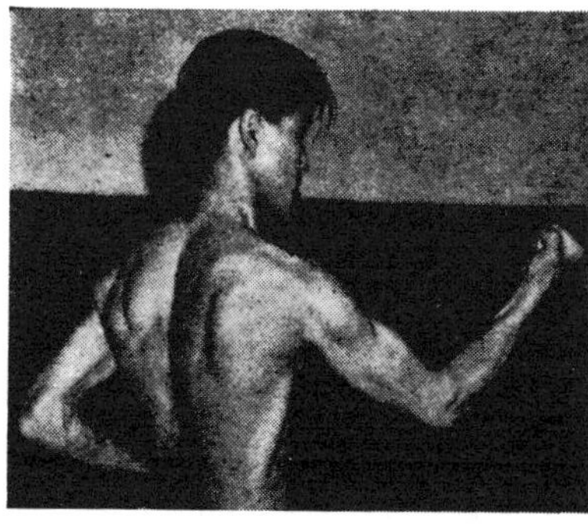

Good

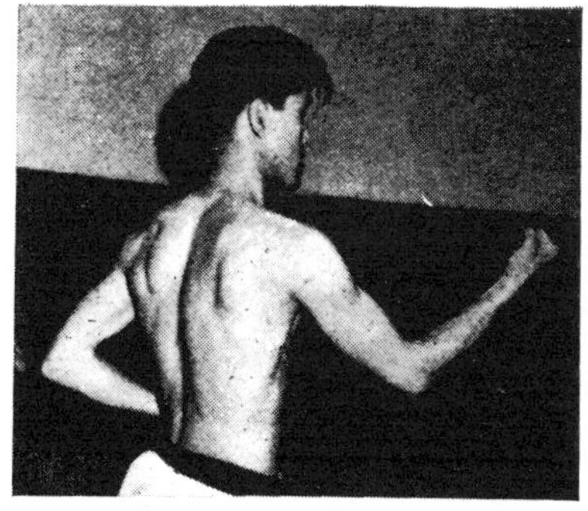

Bad

and by exerting all your energy, you will be able to contract the armpit more and more strongly. The concentration of force which contributes towards strengthening the stomach muscles (saika tanden) makes for a natural Kiai. This is the first step towards what one calls in Karate "striking a blow with the stomach", a terribly effective technique which one does not begin to understand until the 1st Dan black belt stage.

It is a characteristic of the good Karateka to have the armpit strong and contracted, the legs firm and the buttocks taut.

Now, look at the photograph on the previous page and you will see the raised shoulder, empty of force, the decontracted armpit and the total absence of strength in the stomach. All signs of fear.

Followers of cock-fighting know this well, as do those who have observed fighting animals. The frightened young cock raises its wings, lifts itself up on its feet, opens its beak, and breathing is short and rapid. The old champion cock keeps low, with strong wings and head down, and it springs forward . . . and wins. The courageous cat does the same; it crouches and concentrates its strength in the muscles under its legs, while tensing its body and neck. The frightened cat lifts itself on its feet, rounds its back and spits.

For men it is the same. When you are frightened, you raise your shoulders, lift your chin; your breathing is short, you open your mouth and exhale with fear (to the point of crying out involuntarily), your buttocks are slack and the pit of your stomach feels empty. Just the actions to deprive you of energy! In consequence, do exactly the reverse, voluntarily, and you will be suddenly filled with strength and courage. Training will develop these two qualities and in case of grave danger, without underestimating the situation, you will spring to attack or counter attack in full possession of your resources.

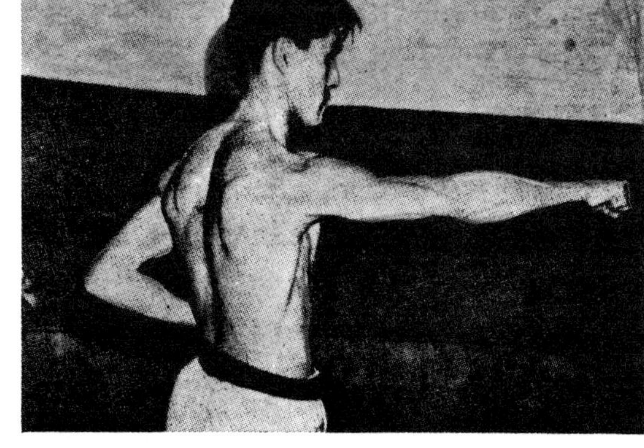

Good
(Concentration)

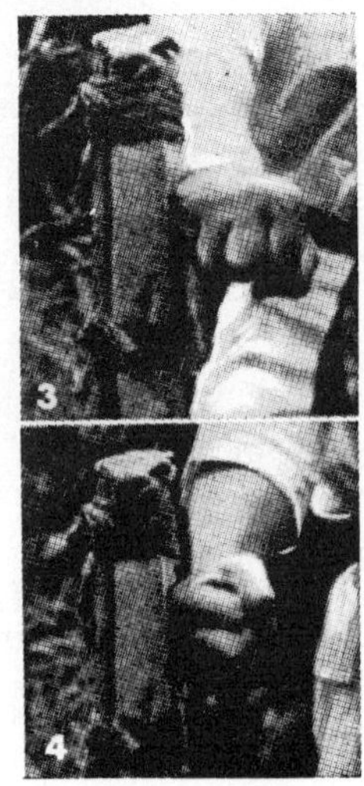

Our Natural Weapons

This little panorama of the possibilities in our hands shows what a pity it is to wrap them up in padded gloves, which limit their capabilities and restrict their use. Here is how to strengthen them.

A. Arms

The Edge of the Hand (Shuto) is demonstrated correctly in Fig. 1. The thumb should simply be folded firmly across the palm to avoid sprains and dislocations. One strikes with the fleshy part of the hand between the little finger and the wrist, the fingers extended but not stiff, as one can see in the top, left-hand photograph on the Makiwara. This is the most common usage (Shuto) together with the side of the thumb (Haito, Fig. 2). One uses it in attack (throat, head, side, etc.) and in defence (blocks against knives, kicks, etc.).

The Finger-Tips (Nukite) is shown in Fig. 6 on page 26. If the attack is made with one finger (index finger to the eye) the other fingers can be folded; if it is made with two fingers, one can join the index and middle fingers and make a fork with the third and fourth, or a fork with the index and middle fingers. If the attack is made with all the fingers, one places the finger-tips in line, bending the top joint of the middle finger to avoid injury. One strikes in this way to the throat or stomach.

The Side of the Fist (Tettsui) is shown correctly in Fig. 3. One strikes with the little finger side of the fist at the temple, nape of the neck, forearm, etc. One can equally well use the inner, thumb side (lower right photograph).

The Back of the Fist (Uraken) is correctly shown in Fig. 4 (one must strike in this way and not as in Fig. 7). One uses the back of the fist near the knuckles of the index and middle fingers, to attack the temples, base of the nose, jaw and any other part of the body.

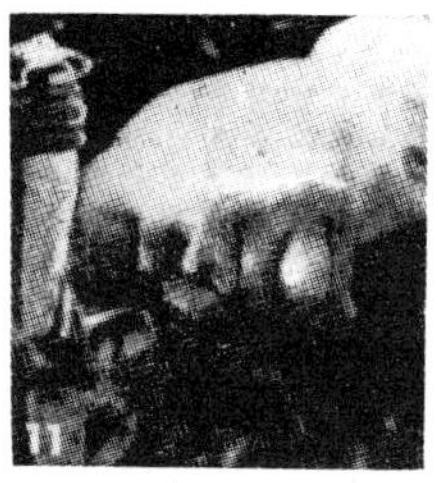

Training on the Makiwara does not take place in the Dojo.
It should be done at home, preferably in the open air.
If you plant the Makiwara in a garden, protect the straw covering with a tin box as in the photograph above.

The Palm (Teisho) is the strong, fleshy part at the base of the palm (see photograph at upper right). One strikes in this way against the temple, jaw, forehead, forearm, chest, pit of the stomach, etc.

The Fist (Seiken) has been described on the previous page (see centre upper photographs). If one is at an average distance, one strikes by turning the hand on impact, nails downwards. If one is close, the hand is not turned (Fig. 7) and the nails are upwards. Between these two ranges, one can keep the fist vertical. There are other ways of using the fist, by extending the second joint of the middle finger, for example (visible in the bottom left photographs and in the top and right) but they are outside the scope of this basic book.

The Elbow (Enpi) is the strongest weapon, but it demands mastery of the most delicate part of Karate, for one must approach very close to the opponent. In attack then, it is only possible from black belt onwards.

B. The Legs

Ball of the Foot (Koshi). It is with this part that one strikes, bare-footed, with speed and power at all parts of the body, including the opponent's arms (when he is taking guard, for example).

The Heel (Kagato or Ensho) is used in side kicks at the side and back.

The Side of the Foot (Sokuto) corresponds to edge of the hand, for kicks to the side and for "Fumikomi" (stamping down on an opponent's instep), etc.

All the other parts of the foot between the knee (for powerful blows) and the toes (with which one can strike equally well) are used in both attack and defence (instep, tops of the toes, etc.). They are, however, outside the scope of this book.

For a period of at least five years up to 2nd-3rd Dan, a Karateka must strengthen his hands by striking against the Makiwara. Following this, he should continue his training on a sack filled with sand, grain, or compressed leather scraps.

As is the case with competitions, it is the mediocre Karateka who are opposed to hardening on the Makiwara or the sack. It is a sign of over-confidence, weakness and a lack of understanding of the true Karate. Of course, to be able to strike the Makiwara with crushing power is not a test of good and true Karate, nor is breaking astounding thicknesses of wood, tiles of earthenware or brick. But to be incapable of delivering sharp, strong and solid blows (without grazing or slipping) is an incontestable sign of a rudimentary technique. In the same way, to be incapable of breaking a reasonable thickness of wood or other material is a sign of a lack of concentration and proper preparation of the natural weapons.

It is absolutely indispensable to practice on the Makiwara with all the natural weapons, and particularly Seiken (Gyaku-Tsuki and Oie-Tsuki). For these are really strong when one has learned to be conscious of the contraction of the internal muscles in the hand and other natural weapons. It is true, then, that in order to progress it is better to train on the sack, so that one may learn more effectively how to strike men. Nevertheless, the Master Yoshitaka Funakoshi practised every day on the Makiwara and the sack, in spite of his high level, and became the greatest genius in Karate. Do not rush matters through pretentiousness. Be modest, serious and reasonable.

Training on the Makiwara

In the photographs above and at the top of the next page, the great Hironishi shows the correct method of training on the Makiwara, in combat position (Gedan-Barai) and striking with Gyaku-Tsuki in the middle level. This is the best method. It is most effective as a counter-attack, for it is very difficult to score a K.O. to the face—Jodan—under 2nd or 3rd Dan. Note the expert posture; this is an intermediary Fudo-Dachi between Kiba Dachi and Zen-Kutsu.

Equally, other attacks can be strengthened in the Kiba-Dachi position (the posture of a man on horseback). It is very good for Shuto, Tettsui, Uraken, Enpi. Note that his posture is low, knees bent at almost 90 degrees. In all the illustrations, particular care should be paid to the opposite arm, withdrawn to its fullest extent with tension and energy (Hikite). This is a sign of a high level of ability. Beginners and less experienced black belts relax the tension when drawing back the arm and let daylight show between the upper arm and the armpit.

Until 1st Dan black belt, and if you have a limited amount of time, it is preferable to train on Seiken in Gyaku-Tsuki only. Place yourself in Ko-Kutsu position, right fist drawn back against the right side, eyes fixed on the Makiwara, left fist closed and held as in Ken-Kutsu on a level with the Makiwara (the fist should not be held too high except in special cases). Concentrate your mind on the Makiwara before striking, most Karateka strike mechanically without real physical power or mental concentration. Then hit and exhale at the same time.

You should resist the recoil of the Makiwara in order to understand its reaction and how to meet it. For this reason, a good Makiwara should be slightly elastic and pliable under the blow. In the beginning, it should preferably be very supple (a ski stick, for example) then it can be stiffened more and more by adding springs or foam rubber behind. This explains how important training is on the Makiwara. That which it teaches cannot be learned in any other way.

34

The Master HIRONISHI Mononobu, whom you can see on the right and at the top of the preceding page, is one of the great experts of modern Japanese Karate. He was a pupil of Master FUNAKOSHI Gichin, and an intimate friend of FUNAKOSHI Yoshitaka (son of the Master) one of the greatest geniuses Karate has known, and who died following exnausting and continuous privations.
One can estimate that there are no more than four survivors among the really great experts after the last World War. Master Hironishi is one of them, together with Master Egami.

With the Hip

When striking, pass from Ko-Kutsu to Zen-Kutsu without raising the hips, with the feeling that you are hitting with the right hip and the abdomen. Put power in the abdomen, keep the shoulder low and the armpit tensed. While delivering the blow, your right elbow brushes against your side, and the other arm brushes against your left side as it is withdrawn to the rear (to balance the blow, the action must be compensated by at least an equivalent force in order to avoid the reaction). This is the only way to concentrate your power.

In the beginning you will certainly skin your knuckles, because instead of hitting cleanly your blows will slip and slide off target, you may even miss altogether and hit the wall. This indicates that your precision is really non-existent. If you are worried about callouses forming on your knuckles, you can put a thin covering of foam rubber or vinyl in front of the straw. This is not important. What matters is that you learn how to tighten the fist correctly on impact, resist the recoil of the Makiwara by putting power into your rear leg and your hip, strike with the hip and abdomen (without pushing your chest forward or advancing the shoulder). Fifty repetitions a day with each hand is the minimum. Practice on the Makiwara is not for the Dojo; it should be carried out at home together with suppling exercises (splits, etc.).

It is desirable to exercise in all the positions. In Kiba-dachi, for example, facing the opponent alternatively with one fist and then the other, without moving the shoulders. Or in Kiba-dachi, sideways on (instead of Ko-Kutsu) and attacking by pivoting the hips while passing into Zen-Kutsu or Fudodachi. Or by advancing in Oie-Tsuki. Or by attacking in Oie-Tsuki from one spot (Mai-Te, in fact) with the advanced fist. Another excellent exercise is to perform Ten-no-Kata from the natural position, without taking the fist back to the hip before striking and when preparing to strike again. This moulds the fist and greatly strengthens the wrist, which always has a tendency to bend. One can also strike with a very quick recoil, or while jumping off the ground (Tobi-Tsuki).

It is necessary to practise regularly and progressively, if not it can produce a minor form of synovitis on the fingers. This is not serious, but it can hold you back for fifteen days. After one month, you will already be competent and after a year you will have a fist strengthened to the point where you can hit a wall without pain.

For certain hardening exercises, one can drive the finger tips into a vase filled with dried beans, which can be replaced by harder materials such as rice, chick peas, etc., according to the degree of progress. It is not very attractive, and I have never liked this training, but it is extremely effective in strengthening the fingers and the mental attitude. One can equally well strike the Makiwara with the finger tips.

You have seen on page 37 how effective the finger tips can be! Terrifying because it can give you an increase in the length of your arm of nearly six inches.

Training with the
Iron Geta

How to consider the Breaking Tests (Shiwari)

The breaking tests which are so spectacular and which leave the onlookers incredulous, are nevertheless genuine. It is not only possible, but it should be within the ability of every black belt Karateka to smash a brick with his bare fist, six inches of wood with the edge of his hand, or twelve inches with his foot, etc. Because every normal man, not specially trained, but able to clench his fist correctly and clear his mind of all inhibitions can equal these exploits. However, it takes at least a year of training to be able to clench the fist correctly, and it is a very difficult matter to obtain at will a pure and impersonal mind. One can understand now why the Karateka feel no anxiety when they make public appeals for an amiable volunteer to break bricks, wood or tiles as they do.

But it is astonishing how many people misunderstand these tests. If anybody can succeed by freeing the mind and striking without fear, by tensing the muscles and tendons so that they can out-hit anyone, it is evident that there must be a special training and a special way of hitting, though different to that necessary to put a human body out of action.

Also, the test of striking or Tame-Shiwari (attempting to strike a blow) is an interesting experience. If one is successful, one gains confidence in the natural weapons and a sort of compensation for the long and monotonous hardening exercises on the Makiwara or the sack.

36

Shiwari performed with the finger-tips (Nukite), shows the power possible with this.

Nevertheless, this is not the objective of Karate. To break five inches of wood or stone shows a certain mastery, but not the "mastery" over body and spirit which is the quest of all philosophies and all religions. It is, after all, nothing more than efficiency . . . for you have to hit an opponent who has no intention of remaining passive.

And to hit an opponent it is necessary to avoid "telegraphing" what you intend to do. This is much more difficult than you might think. It takes many years before one can attack without tell-tale indications in the feet, fists, body, eyes, breathing or in the contraction of the lips, etc. This study of physical purity in action cannot be achieved without a study of mental purity. How can one attack or defend with a pure mind? How can one kill with the sole intention of self protection, and without any feelings of anger or hate in the heart? The contradiction is only apparent. Simply remember that, skill being equal, the victor will be the one with the greatest degree of mental and physical purity. Surely this is one of the most wonderful objectives of Karate?

On these pages you can see several astonishing examples of Tame-Shime, taken from the excellent works "This is Karate" and "Karate, the Art of Empty Hand Fighting" by Oyama and Nishiyama.

The striking tests are not included in the examinations for black belt in Karate.

Gedan-Barai   (Shudan) Ude-Uke   (Shudan) Shuto-Uke

Six Basic Defences

A beginner, that is to say, a practitioner of black belt grade and under, has relatively few techniques that he must know:—

—Six blocks, which are at the same time disengagements and attacks, performed at several levels against attacks by the hands or the feet.

—Four attacks with the feet, performed at three or four heights and in two ways: penetrating (Ke-Komi) or a percussive, upwards action (Ke-Age).

—Two attacks with the fist at three heights (Oie-Tsuki and Gyaku-Tsuki) to attack or counter attack.

—All these in three basic postures. Great attention must be paid to maintaining the weight equally between the feet and to keeping a natural posture.

Principal Defences and Attacks in Karate

BASIC BLOCKS

Gedan-Barai: Two heights, sweeping downwards.

Ude-Uke: Two heights, interior block towards the exterior forearm (or Uchi-Uki).

Shuto-Uke: Two heights, block with the edge of the hand.

Shuto-Barai: Two heights, defence with the edge of the hand against a grip.

Age-Uke: One height, a sweeping, upward block.

Uchi-Komi: Two heights, sweep with the exterior forearm towards the inside while coming in close (also called Soto-Uke but without coming in).

SOME OTHER BLOCKS

Uchi-Barai: (or Gedan-Uchi-Uke), sweeping an attack with the foot from the interior to the exterior.

Moro-Uke: Two heights, a stronger block interior to exterior.

Juji-Uke: Block with the two hands crossed, open or closed, high or low.

Kakiwake-Uke: Double block with the hands widely separated.

Tsuki-Uke: Block while attacking with a high punch.

Teisho-Uke: Block or sweep with the base of the palm.

Keito-Uke: Block with the base of the thumb.

Kakuto-Uke: Block from above with the wrist curved (generally high).

Haishu-Uke: Block against the chest with the open hand.

Tettsui-Uke: Block while striking with the side of the fist.

Kake-Uke: High block with the wrist while reversing the attack.

Bukami-Uke: Block while taking hold to pull off balance.

Nagashi-Uke: Sideways block while sweeping with the palm of the hand.

(Jodan) Shuto-Barai   (Jodan) Age-Uke

Four Basic Attacks with the Feet

Osae-Uke: Downward block with the palm while holding in position (or Shitei-Soto, Uchi and Gedan-Uke).

Uchi-Uke-Gedan-Barai: Double block with both hands at the same time.

Shuto-Uchi-Uke: Block with the edge of the hand, of the Ude-Uchi-Uke type.

Shuto-Soto-Uke: Block with the edge of the hand from the exterior towards the interior, of the Soto-Uke type.

Basic Foot Attacks

Mae-Geri: Direct kick at two levels.

Yoko-Geri: Sideways kick at two heights.

Mawashi-Geri: Whipping, circular kick at two heights.

Ushiro-Geri: Kick to the rear at two heights.

Some Other Attacks with the Feet

Mae-Geri-Keage: Direct, upward kick.

Yoko-Geri-Keage: Upward kick to the side.

Mawashi-Uchi: Circular kick to the inside (exterior to interior).

Ushiro-Geri-Keage: Upward kick to the rear.

Mikazuki-Geri: Semi-circular kick with the sole of the foot.

Fumikomi: Two forms for stamping on an opponent.

Mae-Tobi-Geri: Direct, jumping kick.

Nidan-Geri: Double kick in two stages.

Yoko-Tobi-Geri: Jumping kick to the side.

Kin-Geri: Direct, upward kick to the groin.

Hittsui-Geri: Two forms of striking with the knee.

Kansetsu-Geri: Kick to dislocate the knee.

Ushiro-Mawashi: Circular kick to the rear.

Kakato-Geri: Kick with the heel (two forms).

Nami-Ashi: Internal counter to a low attack.

Mikazuki-Geri-Uke: External counter to an attack.

Kubi-Geri: Circular kick with the top of the foot.

Gyaku-Tsuki   Gyaku-Tsuki-Tsukomi

1

2

3

4

Basic Attacks with the Fist
Oie-Tsuki: Pursuing attack with fist and foot (or Jun-Tsuki).
Gyaku-Tsuki: Attack contrary to the foot.

Some Other Attacks with the Hand
Jun-Tsuki-Tsukomi: Oie-Tsuki from a stooping position.
Tobikomi-Tsuki: Oie-Tsuki while jumping forward.
Gyaku-Tsuki-Tsukomi: Gyaku-Tsuki from a stooping position.
Tobi-Tsuki: Oie-Tsuki while jumping.
Tikikomi-Tsuki: Attack with the advanced fist, jumping forward.
Maete-Tsuki: (or Age-Tsuki) Attack with the advanced fist.
Morote-Tsuki: Attack with two fists at the same time, or one fist reinforced by the other.
Age-Tsuki: Upward blow.
Mawashi-Tsuki: Semi-circular swing (as in boxing).
Ura-Tsuki: Blow with the fist turned, nails upwards (uppercut).
Tate-Tsuki: Blow with the fist straight, nails sideways (straight punch in boxing).
Yama-Tsuki: Double attack at two levels.
Bari-Bari-Tsuki: A "one-two" attack, as in boxing.
Kagi-Tsuki: Hook.
Riken-Uchi: or Uraken, blow with the back of the closed fist.
Uraken-Shomen-Uchi: Blow with the back of the fist to the front.
Tettsui-Uchi: Attack with the side of the fist (Gedan-Barai).
Shuto-Uchi: Direct attack with the edge of the hand.
Shuto-Sakotsu-Uchikomi: Thrusting blow with the edge of the hand.
Haito-Uchi: Blow with the edge of the hand inwards and upwards.
Haishu-Uchi: Back of the hand.
Teisho-Uchi: Blow with the palm of the hand in an upwards direction.
Enpi-Uchi: Elbow.

All these other attacks derive from specific and basic attacks. Among them are the following:
Nukite (finger-tips).
Ippon-Ken (fist with the knuckles of the index finger protruding).
Nakadate-Ippon-Ken (fist with the knuckle of the middle finger protruding).
Hiraken (with the phalanges).
Kumade (gripping with the hand).
Koko (edge of the index finger).
Kakuto ("swan neck", etc.).

Karate is very rich in attacks and defences with the hands and feet. One can count 160 different attacks and defences, all very effective and practical (pokes, backward kicks, etc.). But if one is content to concentrate on the classic bases, progress in the other attacks will be easy and rapid. All the valid attacks and defences have the same secrets. "To know" is less important than "To rediscover". The enthusiastic beginner must be reasonable enough to learn how to control himself, to work intelligently without wasting time, and not to squander his efforts in a search for illusory satisfactions. If you have the courage, try to rediscover the secrets contained in every attack and every defence; there are realities in them and very important ones. Do not think that a Master, admired by everyone, is necessarily stupid and limited because he spends ten years repeating nothing but Mae-Geri and Oie-Tsuki or a single Kata. Think rather the reverse. Chudan-Uchi-Uke and Chudan-Soto-Uke are frequently called just "Ude-Uke" in Japan (see pages 55 and 63).

40

Basic Postures
Zen-Kutsu: advanced leg bent, upper part of the body square or in profile.
Ko-Kutsu: rear leg bent, upper part of the body in profile (or Hanmi-No-Nekoashi).
Kiba-Dachi: "horseman's" posture (or Naifanchi-Dachi).
Other Postures
Heisoku-Dachi: alert posture with feet together.
Musubi-Dachi: alert posture with heels together (or Fudo-No-Shisei).
Hachiji-Dachi: alert posture with legs wide apart (or Yoi-No-Shisei, or Heiko-Dachi).
Uchihachi-Ji-Dachi: alert posture with toes inwards.
Shiko-Dachi: as Kiba-Dachi with toes turned outwards.
Sanchin-Dachi: natural, lateral posture with knees inwards.
Hangetsu-Dachi: Sanchin-Dachi, but wider.
Fudo-Dachi: intermediate between Kiba and Zen-Kutsu (or Sochin-Dachi).
Neko-Ashi-Dachi: "cat" posture, tighter form of Ko-Kutsu.
Hanmi: Ko-Kutsu, one leg slightly advanced.
Hanmi-No-Nekoashi: Ko-Kutsu with upper part of the body three-quarter turned.
Tsuruashi-Dachi: "Heron" posture.
Kake-Dachi: posture with legs crossed.
Moroashi-Dachi: natural posture with one leg advanced.

Successive Attacks and Combinations in the Striking Movements

Successive attacks and combinations in the striking movements (some combination principles)
The table below gives the principal combinations in the striking movements, seen from the
point of view of general theory and not just in terms of "natural weapons" which one finds
generally.

Simple striking attack

- (1st) with an advanced limb (fist or foot) it is very fast but rather weak.
- (2nd) with the rear fist or leg, very strong, but can be blocked or countered because of the length of the movement.
- (3rd) with the head.

Striking attacks with the same limb (two or more times) at the same level or at different levels.

- (1st) with the advanced limb in succession without drawing the fist or leg back between the blows (in the latter case the foot is not placed back on the ground after the first blow).
- (2nd) with the rear limb, drawing the fist back or replacing the foot on the ground after each blow (this gives the opponent confidence and causes him to expose himself to the second attack).
- (3rd) with the head in succession.

Alternate striking attacks with two limbs (at the same level or at different levels).

- (1st) with the upper limbs (left, right) or the lower limbs (left, right).
- (2nd) with an upper advanced limb followed by a lower advanced limb.
- (3rd) with an upper advanced limb followed by a lower rear limb.
- (4th) with an upper rear limb followed by a lower advanced limb.
- (5th) with an upper rear limb followed by an upper rear limb.
- (6th) with a lower advanced limb followed by an upper advanced limb.
- (7th) with a lower advanced limb followed by an upper rear limb.
- (8th) with a lower rear limb followed by an upper advanced limb.
- (9th) with a lower rear limb followed by an upper rear limb.
- (10th) attack with an advanced or rear limb followed by a blow with the head.

Striking attacks with two limbs at the same time.

- (1st) the two upper limbs in a forward direction at the same time, the advanced arm can be crossed over the other, or uncrossed.
- (2nd) the two upper limbs at the same time to the side (generally in Kiba-Dachi).
- (3rd) the two lower limbs at the same time in a forward direction (by jumping or putting the hands on the ground).
- (4th) the two lower limbs at the same time to the side (by jumping or putting the hands on the ground).

Striking attacks while jumping (acrobatics—sometimes risky

- (1st) with the two lower limbs at the same time (see above).
- (2nd) with the two lower limbs alternately to the front and side (Nidan-Keri, Yoko-Tobikeri etc.).
- (3rd) with the lower limbs to complete an attack with one or both hands (Sankaku-Tobi, a jumping attack from three angles).

against a single opponent, but very useful in serious combat against several opponents or to break out of a circle).

(4th) a jumping attack behind a single extended limb, with the idea in mind of sacrificing yourself (Tobi-Tsuki, Tobi-Mae-Keri, etc.) a very effective means of getting above an attack, a kick, a blow with a stick, etc., but demands a high level of skill.

(5th) a plunging, jumping attack with a single limb in order to get under a normal or jumping attack against you (Ushiro-Geri, Mae-Keri which is rather like Tomoe-Nage in Judo, a blow with the shoulder against the knees, etc.).

In fact, the complete range of combinations is an impressive one if you take into account:
1. the number of natural weapons of the body is more than 25;
2. each attack by an upper or lower limb can be direct (Tsuki, Nukite, Mae-Keri, etc.), upwards (Age-Tsuki, Ke-Age), descending (Tetsu, Enpi, etc.), hooking (Mawashi-Keri and Mawashi-Uchi, etc.), and every striking or penetrating (Kekomi) movement according to the place to be attacked and the objects of research.

Very often, the Karateka remains attached to the absorbing subject of self-mastery, but the application of strategies and combinations allow of a different sort of mastery for they give a feeling of adaptation to the outside world. Introverted research brings doubtful benefits if one neglects the studies outwards, to the relations with nature and the universe. This may sound elevated and pretentious, but perhaps you will remember it one day.

It must be understood that my sole aim is to help you, and if I have attained a certain mastery over all the matters dealt with in this book, I do not go so far as to pretend that I have achieved a complete mastery or even a superior one.

Please give me credit for having a rather greater sense of reality.

This rare and excellent photograph of the Master Yoshitaka Funakoshi (son of Master Gichin), shows all his class, and those who know what to look for will appreciate his combat position.
Below one can see the difference in the case of quite reputable Karateka. The difficulty is spontaneous application and strategy without losing the basic qualities (hips strong and low, etc.).

A Table of Combat Applications and Strategies

Many Karateka who are proud of their own ability are, unfortunately, still in the elementary stage. Sometimes, they have still to reach the elementary stage! For example, they are not yet capable of unbalancing the opponent with a block or putting him out of action with a single movement (Master Yoshitaka Funakoshi once eliminated a "Champion" in this way who had come to Okinawa to challenge his father's Dojo: with one block at face level, he broke the fore-arm, ulnar and radius . . .). One very rarely sees this block followed by an immediate counter attack (But how many Karateka have simply one clear, theoretical idea of the usable strategies and the combinations? If you are in doubt, here is a brief table which will enlighten you. Obviously there is a wide gap between theory and practice. One cannot describe many of the subtleties for they have a "tempo", a rhythm, which varies according to the opponent's reactions and which can only be taught by close, personal involvement.

1st GROUP **SEN** Initiative = Use of your own efforts.	(A) To execute a straightforward technique which puts the opponent out of action, by speed or by taking advantage of an opportunity.	(1st) By a blow. (2nd) By a block. (3rd) By pressure. (4th) By a throw. (5th) By a lock. (6th) By strangulation.
	(B) Starting from one technique in order to achieve a similar one (blow—> blow, throw —> throw, etc.).	(1st) In the same direction. (2nd) From left to right or right to left. (3rd) From front to rear. (4th) From rear to front.
	(C) Starting from one technique in order to achieve a different one (blow—> throw, blow—> dislocation, blow—> strangulation.)	(1st) Producing loss of balance to the rear. (2nd) Producing a loss of balance to the front. (3rd) Producing a loss of balance to the side (and all the intermediary positions).
2nd GROUP Using the efforts and actions of the opponent. **SEN-NO-SEN** Initiative countered by initiative. **GO-NO-SEN** Countering an initiative.	(A) Counter a technique by a similar one (blow —> blow, throw—> throw, etc.) (the principles opposite are equally valid for countering certain attacks by different techniques).	(1st) By taking advantage of the momentary weakness at the start of the opponent's attack (it is necessary for him to decontract slightly at this time, therefore you should anticipate or start after him but make sure that you land first with your blow, throw, etc.). This is the ideal in all the MARTIAL ARTS, and is called SEN-NO-SEN. (2nd) By taking advantage of the momentary weakness at the end of an attack which has miscarried. (3rd) By taking advantage of his effort while you evade or deflect his attack (either by accentuating his momentary loss of balance, or by using his force to increase the power of your own attack force against force). (4th) By controlling his technique (through evasion of his effort before it has been completed, either by gripping him, or by blocking).
	(B) Counter a blow with a close quarters technique.	(1st) Evade or block and follow up at close quarters in a standing position (lock, strangulation, compressing a nerve centre). (2nd) As above, but follow up with a close quarters attack on the ground (immobilization, lock, strangulation, throw him by hurling yourself at his legs, etc.).
	(C) Counter a close quarters attack with a close quarters counter-attack.	(1st) By striking a blow just as the opponent is taking hold. (2nd) By a blow as you control him (during a throw, a lock or a strangulation). (3rd) By a blow to finish a close quarters struggle (on the ground, from underneath, etc.). (1st) A standing close quarters attack against a standing close quarters attack. (2nd) A standing close quarters attack against a close quarters attempt to take you to the ground. (3rd) On being taken to the ground, you counter with a close quarters attack.

This is, in fact, the whole ART OF KARATE. The study of the movements, their co-ordination, the "fortification" of the body, these are just the preparation. Except when one searches for a form of interior mastery comparable to religious meditation. This is no longer exactly Karate, for one can verify this mastery only by application. Otherwise there is no point in Karate, there are certainly other less difficult disciplines.

2

DETAILED DESCRIPTION
OF THE BASIC ATTACKS BLOCKS POSTURES

The wonderful efficacy of Master Yoshitaka Funakoshi is demonstrated here.
You will find many other pictures of Master Yoshitaka in the section on Sanbon-
Kumites which appears later in this book.

The Four Fundamental Attacks with the Foot
—MAWASHI-GERI: circular, whipping kick.　　—MAE-GERI: direct kick to front.
—YOKO-GERI: kick to side.—USHIRO-GERI: kick to rear (with heel or edge of foot).
It is difficult to explain in a few words the finer points of kicking. It is very hard to strike with
really devastating force using the foot. A great deal of training is necessary against an imaginary
target and on the bag (NEVER on the makiwara) raising the toes as much as possible. In nearly
all the foot attacks, the leg must be withdrawn after impact at a greater speed than that of the
initial attack. The heel of the supporting leg must never leave the ground (always imagine that
you are on a very slippery surface). The knee of the supporting leg must therefore be bent to a
greater or lesser degree according to the height of the kick (low, middle or high). The shoulders
must remain as square as possible, and the backward inclination of the upper part of the body
must be kept to the minimum. The whole mind and body must be concentrated in the direction
of the opponent, without, however, losing balance.

Mae-Geri

For MAE-GERI: you raise the knee as high and as quickly as possible in front of the chest
(for defence, and also for training in knee attacks), toes raised, and strike as far in front of you
as possible. It is better to train a great deal on kicks at belt level than to strike high but without
effect. Bring the foot back in front of you, or behind you, or in front while advancing (if the
opponent retreats). One can also train by kicking several times without putting the foot back
on the ground in order to gain stability.

Yoko-Geri

For YOKO-GERI: you start from the Zen-Kutsu position (Fig. 11) or Kiba-Dachi.
In this case you cross one leg in front or behind you and raise the knee in front of the chest.
At the same time, you strike sideways with the heel and then bring the foot immediately back
to its original position (ready to begin again, or to place the foot to your rear, to the side or in
front of you, according to the opponent's movements). Ideally, the foot and knee of the
supporting leg must not move. It is a magnificent "stopping" movement. As in all attacks, the
three movements must become as one.

Mawashi-Geri

For MAWASHI-GERI: you must, as the Japanese name indicates, kick in a roundabout,
circular, way. Starting from the Zen-Kutsu position (forward leg bent), you raise the knee and
strike the opponent in the stomach, the face, the lower abdomen, the kidneys or the back of the
knee, when he is sideways on and well protected. You should strike with the ball of the foot,
the tips of the toes (there are several tricks for placing them), or with the instep (foot extended)
with the idea in mind of driving it right through the opponent (this is ideal for following up
with a punch or a blow with the elbow).
If the opponent defends or counter-attacks, you can return to your original position.
This attack is perfectly horizontal and even slightly downwards.

Ushiro-Geri

For USHIRO-GERI: you raise your leg as in Yoko-Geri and kick as far as possible to the rear,
with the heel or the edge of the foot. At the same time, you should look back under your
shoulder in order to follow the action. It is an effective attack, but slow and dangerous in Shiai
or serious combat. It allows you to defend yourself unexpectedly against a second adversary.
As with all the blocks and arm attacks, when striking with the feet do not let the shoulders,
elbows, head or arms wobble. The hips must stay on the same level while moving forward
or to the rear. Never take your eyes off your opponent. Concentrate your strength in the
muscles under your armpits, in your abdomen and legs (this is just a beginning), otherwise
you will never be able to block or parry a really strong attack, or to deliver a blow with the
fist or foot which will finish the fight there and then. This is the ideal in Karate.

46

Mae-Geri

Yoko-Geri

Mawashi-Geri

Ushiro-Geri

The Four Basic Postures and The Two Basic Attacks

Hachi-Dachi (or Yoi-no-Shisei)

As with all simple things, this posture is really one of the most difficult (as one can understand by the Ten-no-Kata). The literal translation is "posture of readiness" but is generally called "waiting posture". Jump up and down a few times on one spot; your body will naturally assume the correct position and your feet will take up the proper separation. Then stop and stay just where you are. Put your strength in your abdomen, in your armpits, your buttocks and legs. Clench your fists strongly, then relax the strength in your fists without letting them open. Carry them slightly away from your body, or else along your thighs (this is a question of personal temperament). Look straight ahead far in front of you, attentively, with quiet breathing and your chin drawn in, You will feel, at one and the same time, both heavy and light, strong and fast. while being partially relaxed. As in all the other Karate postures.

Yoi-Dachi
(Waiting Posture)

Zen-Kutsu-Dachi

The translation means "bending forward posture" (in Karate, the trunk is kept upright while advanced). From 50 per cent to 60 per cent of your weight is carried on the advanced leg, which should be firm and deeply flexed (the knee in line with the big toe). The rear leg should be strong and extended. In trying to achieve greater strength in the hips, black belts can sometimes flex the rear leg slightly, thereby obtaining a compromise between two positions. But students should not try to imitate them. The distance between the legs should be the full width of the hips for beginners, and, as one progresses, it can be narrowed to about six inches. The toes of the leading foot should be turned inwards slightly; the rear foot, heel on the ground, should point forwards at an angle of about 20 per cent to 45 per cent. Without wishing to dishearten you, I must warn you that it is from two to five years before you understand and get the feeling of Zen-Kutsu-Dachi, as is the case with the other postures also.

Ko-Kutsu-Dachi (Hanmi-no-Nekoashi)

The translation means "posture with the body turned sideways, the heel of the advanced foot clear of the ground". The rear leg carries from 60 per cent to 80 per cent of your body weight (according to the amount of weight carried on the rear leg and the degree to which the hips are turned, depend the variations such as Neko-Ashi, Mahami-no-Nekoashi, Hidari-Hanmi, etc.). With these also, the rear foot should be flat on the ground and pointing forward at an angle of 20 per cent to 45 per cent. The advanced foot, heel clear of the ground, points forward in line with the rear foot. The rear leg must be deeply flexed; this may seem very difficult at first, but you must persevere and strive for solidity. This posture is frequently practised in defence (it is easy to deliver a stop-kick with the advanced leg), but it can also be a very good posture for attack as is Zen-Kutsu, in principle the most useful of all for attack. Can be excellent in defence.

Heisoku Dachi	Fudo-No Shisei	Yoi-No Shisei	Hachiji-Dachi	Shiko-Dachi	Kiba-Dachi or Naifanchi-Dachi

Zen-Kutsu-Dachi (for Attack)   Fudo-Dachi (Counter-Attack)   Ko-Kutso-Dachi (Defence)

Kiba-Dachi

The translation is "horseback posture" (and Tekki: "iron horseman"). The body weight is carried by both legs, which should be deeply flexed, and the toes turned inwards as if you were riding a horse. The strength must therefore be in the inside of the thighs. It is one of the strongest postures. Beginners may not find it very interesting, but according to their degree of progress they will understand its significance. Black belts practise it a great deal, for it assists progress and strengthens the legs and hips. Do not let the stomach or buttocks protrude. This posture is generally used sideways or three-quarter on to attack or to counter-attack. Take a stop-watch in your hand and hold the position for long time to drive out your mental weaknesses: anybody can hold a position with knees bent at an angle of 90 degrees for an hour, at will, and for three hours under duress (behind a machine-gun, for example). Well? How long can you keep it up? Take notice if you tremble, cry out with pain or if it brings tears to your eyes—hold it! This is the mental aspect of Karate. There is no point in beginning the test again afterwards, after one or two years you will know that you can do it, and you will not trouble yourself with other techniques quite so much.

If the advanced foot is turned as in Zen-Kutsu, you will obtain the position of Fudo-Dachi or "motionless posture" which is used by Black Belts skilled in Ten-no-Kata. If both feet are turned outwards instead of inwards, you will obtain the Shika-Dachi position, a posture very well known in Sumo wrestling circles.

Combat Posture

One generally takes the Zen-Kutsu combat position when performing GEDAN-BARAI (sweeping defence with the arm), photograph above: (a) by stepping back if you are too close to the opponent, and (b) by advancing if he is too far away. At the finish of Gedan-Barai you should be in perfect fighting range, and if necessary, you can move forward a little to make sure.

Oie-Tsuki (Attack)

The OIE-TSUKI attack (a straight punch with the fist as a "follow-up", Fig. 1, page 38) consists of a blow, for example with the right fist, after having advanced the right foot. At the same time, you rapidly withdraw the other fist turning the hand (nails upwards) as you do so. The chest should be almost square on at impact. You must not slap the foot down, or drag it

Mahanmi-No Nekoashi	Ko-Kutsu or Hanmi-No-Necoashi	Neko-ashi	Hidari-Hanmi	Zen-Kutsu

on the ground, or move it heavily, or make hesitant, warning movements. One can attack equally well in this way while retreating.

OIE-TSUKI is one of the best possible attacks possible in a fight where you run the risk of being counter-attacked by a kick (it is the only one to use in Ju-Ippon-Kumite up to 1st Dan). Being out of reach of a kick, a distance which is called "Ma", and which varies according to the opponent's technique, it is necessary to leap one or more yards into the opponent or into his attack. While advancing, your knees should be close together to protect your lower abdomen, without raising your hips or your head (the attack must be as straight as an arrow). The feet should be placed as far apart as the width of your hips, then according to the degree of progress, this distance can be reduced to about six inches and finally in line after 1st or 2nd Dan.

Gyaku-Tsuki (Counter-Attack)

In GYAKU-TSUKI (an attack "contrary" to the legs, see Fig. 4 page 39) one strikes with the right fist while the left foot is advanced, and vice versa. The shoulders are also square on at impact. This is an ideal attack after blocking. Gyaku-Tsuki is therefore more a pure counter-attack (see illustration above). But if the opponent retreats during your Gyaku-Tsuki, you can follow up and turn it into an Oie-Tsuki. One can say, therefore, that Oie-Tsuki is a continuation of Gyaku-Tsuki. Gyaku-Tsuki can equally well be an attack if the distance permits; some schools raise the heel of the rear leg if the range is long.

The Real Beginner—The First Dan

Up to black belt a Karateka is a beginner. He learns the movements of attack and defence, the technical bases, the order of certain Katas, and he strengthens his body and his will. But though he "knows" he does not yet "understand", and above all, he has not yet "mastered" or instinctively "felt" the technique or the spirit of Karate. Many errors are committed before black belt, the greatest of which is self-satisfaction. For a child to know the alphabet does not mean that he is immediately in a position to rival the great authors.

After black belt, the Karateka has a clear vision of the road ahead. He has laid the foundations, and this is no mere figure of speech, it takes several years to form strong legs and they are the real foundations. It remains for him to build, then to improve. It takes on an average from one and a half years (two to three hours training daily) to three years (two hours training twice a week) to earn 1st Dan. On the nervous plane, this relates to the studies carried out recently by the police, according to which it requires one and a half years of educative driving to cut the average motorist's reaction time by half.

How to Block

Blocking an attack is an easy matter in theory, but difficult in practice. Because, in order for it to succeed, it is necessary to advance into the attack or at least remain at a proper distance. Now instinct makes you retreat, even quite a long way. Therefore, one sees very few real blocks or sweeps in the Ju-Kumites (free, supple contests). This has the consequence of greatly limiting the number of attacks and counter-attacks with the fist, the most effective in serious combat under any conditions.

The Karateka training intelligently must struggle unceasingly against the weaknesses and shortcomings which come from the instinct of self-preservation, and channel them and turn them into advantages.

That is to say, he must strive from the very beginning never to let an opponent's attack go by without blocking with all his strength whether the attack is good or bad (not strong enough, not close enough, etc.). He must think of throwing the opponent off balance. Then, as he rises in grade, never to block without counter-attacking (fist in Gyaku or fist followed by foot). Then gradually to reduce the time interval between block and counter-attack so that the whole

50

Techniques are classified in three heights, depending on whether one is defending against an attack above the level of the shoulders, between the shoulders and the belt, or below the belt:
—Face (JODAN Jo: high, Dan: level).
—Stomach (CHUDAN, Chu: middle).
—Lower abdomen and legs (GEDAN, Ge: low).

Karate, like swimming, is a natural reflex action lost through human civilisation (all animals can swim except man); one can rediscover it with difficulty, but it is no longer lost above a certain level of physical and mental mastery (physical co-ordination and the disappearance of ancestral fears).

action becomes one, single movement. Then attack more and more with the fist as a first move, rather than with the foot as one is always tempted to do. Afterwards, when the blocks are strong and instinctive, the fist attacks fast, controlled and powerful, he must endeavour to make progress in the speed and power of the leg attacks and always follow them up with an attack with the fist. Then, and on this level only, he can attack first with the foot, for this attack will always and automatically be followed by the fist.

It is then that he will begin to follow up with blows delivered with the elbow, with throws, with double attacks (both fists at once or foot and fist at once, etc.) and . . . he will be performing real Karate.

Applying the True Aim of Karate

This is the aim of training. The aim of Karate. In effect, the true aim of Karate is to give its practitioners the greatest possible chances of winning. In a life or death struggle, the combatants always start off with equal chances, whatever their technique. Many a time boxing champions have been knocked out by amateurs without the slightest knowledge of the sport. Only training, and in particular Karate training, can reduce this uncertainty if it is carried out intelligently. One must never underestimate an opponent or a training partner. One must always train with the idea in mind that even at an advanced age, one may have to save one's life by Karate, and consequently one must beware of those successes due to youth alone. Without technical knowledge, young people can beat others in a rough and tumble in the gymnasium fairly easily if they are better trained. But youth passes, say at 20 to 35 years, and then they will have nothing left. Karate has nobler and deeper aims than a rough and tumble. A true Karateka never ceases to progress as he grows older, even though he does not perform so many "Ju-Kumites", and it is here that one finds an important difference in comparison with other combat sports, such as boxing, where one rarely sees first-class boxers continuing their training, or even keeping in form, once the first flush of youth has gone.

One must never forget this when beginning Karate, and it can be said that no real progress can be made if one does not start with the firm determination to continue studying until one's dying breath.

The Kihon
The frequent execution of blocks is extremely important, not only for improving the reflexes but because it strengthens the legs, fists, arms and the sides, and teaches one to parry all attacks instinctively, even those below the level of the stomach, when one is well trained.
The best training for blocking is the exercise called "Kihon", in space (against an imaginary opponent) either on one spot or in movement. Afterwards, it is necessary to practise them with a partner . . . otherwise it is not Karate.

The Kumites
"Kumite" means an encounter (Kumi) with the hands (Te) in free combat.
There are many types of Kumite in Karate, with different mental attitudes and different objectives, but it is necessary to remember but four in order to attain black belt.

Gohon-Kumite
This is an exercise repeated five times (Go, five; Hon, times). One generally makes five attacks, for example with the right fist, then the left, the right, the left and finally, the right. The opponent defends himself each time without counter-attacking (but with an irresistible desire to do so) and after the fifth attack, he launches his own counter. One usually advances five steps while attacking; this obliges the defender (Uke) to retreat accordingly. Each attack must be clearly defined, as if it were the only one. If space permits, one can precede Gohon-Kumite with Juhon-Kumite (ten attacks). It is a good thing to accompany each attack and each defence with a Kiai.

Sanbon-Kumite
Having progressed, one can reduce the number to three (San). But this time one attacks three times very quickly and completely, beginning always with the right fist, generally while making three changes of position. One single Kiai for the three attacks. The defender (Uke) does his best to avoid the attacks (he can also turn) and to unbalance his opponent so that he can maintain control for his own counter on the third attack. If he is too far away to counter with the fist (preferably at middle level) he can use the foot and follow up with the fist. As in Gohon, the attacks in Sanbon-Kumite must be REAL (genuine risk of a K.O.) *but* at a level indicated BEFORE the Kumite. This is an indispensable condition for the progress of both.
On pages 53, 55, 57, 59, 61, and 63 you can see the application of the six basic blocks (of the Ten-no-Kata) in Sanbon-Kumite.

Ippon-Kumite
Having made further progress one can reduce to one attack (Ippon). While in Gohon and Sanbon the defender (Uke) takes up a natural posture and the attacker a fighting posture (right Zen-Kutsu), in Ippon-Kumite, both adopt the most favourable posture. This can be Yoi-Dachi (feet parallel) or Zen-Kutsu or another. They can move freely while trying to find the correct distance Mae) in the beginning, but there must be only ONE ATTACK (the Karate ideal). This can be a "decision" attack, that is to say, a successive attack, but as soon as the attacker has been countered the combat ends. The partners salute each other and start again. If they continue in this way, it becomes a Ju-Kumite (free practice combat) where the number of victories or defeats has no significance . . . by reason of the dishonesty of those who, though beaten, sometimes continue to attack because they have not actually been hit.

Ju-Kumite
In effect, one should deliver real blows in Gohon, Sanbon, Ippon-Kumite because the opponent knows exactly where and how often he is going to be attacked. But in Ju-Kumite, as is often not realised, all the attacks must be controlled. Needless to say, the counter-attacks must never even graze the opponent (as in Gohon, Sanbon and Ippon). The object of this exercise is to give a sense of combat before the attack has come to a head. It is consequently on a lower level to Ippon-Kumite, which is a search for perfect efficacy.

GEDAN-BARAI

GEDAN-BARAI is one of the best ways of defending oneself against kicks or other blows (with the fists, etc. see Figs. 1 and 2) below the level of the belt. It can also be a very effective way of releasing a grip on the wrist (Figs. 3, 4 and 5). Performed on the outside of the arm, it can break or dislocate the elbow of the attacker who strikes a blow or grips you.

Starting from the on-guard position, you cross the arms (right hand nails close to your ear) and strike with the outside of the fist just after having stepped your left foot forward in Zen-Kutsu (Zen: forward, Kutsu: crouch). At the same time you draw your left fist very quickly back towards your left hip.

At the end of the position, your right fist is about nine inches above your knee, which is deeply flexed. Your left leg is strong and extended to the rear. Your right foot is slightly turned inwards, your left foot is pointed forwards with the sole flat on the ground. That is to say, in correct Zen-Kutsu.

It is very important to repeat this movement time and time again with great speed and power, so as to be able to do it without constraint, with a spontaneous suppleness, moving forwards and backwards, to the right and to the left.

Gedan-Barai (Sweeping block downwards)   Soto-Gedan-Barai   Uchi-Gedan-Barai

The Dojo and the "Sensei"

You must comport yourself better in the Dojo than anywhere else, because that is why you go there. You must concentrate on what you are doing, and do it with decision and energy, without ever avoiding the difficulties. You must be clean, your finger and toe nails cut short, your feet washed BEFORE EVERY training session; some even take a shower before training in a spirit of self-purification. You must not talk during training. Outside the Dojo you can be gay, make as much noise as you like, but always without coarseness and avoiding racial or religious subjects. Never walk in the Dojo with your shoes on, or in a state of undress. You should not drink alcohol, or smoke (even in the immediate vicinity) except in special circumstances (reunions, seniors' dinners, etc.).

In the Dojo, you must show great respect to the seniors. You must salute the Seat of Honour (Joseki), or the "Sensei", or the most senior man present when entering or leaving. This hierarchy is very important, for only the seniors can enable you to make progress. One can show you in the course of several years of normal Karate, new movements, the Katas WITHOUT YOU MAKING PROGRESS. The feeling of true Karate can only be transmitted by those whom you respect and for whom you feel affection. Not to salute the seniors, not to assist them (carry their Keikogi, for example) not to give them your best wishes (at New Year, anniversaries or fetes) is not just impolite, it is stupid.

You must have CONFIDENCE in your instructors. If you criticise what they teach you, if you call them into question, you can be assured that they will not insist. DO NOT KEEP A CLOSED MIND, because you will reject everything a priori without even having worked. In the same way, when the instructor tells you to attack you must do so whole-heartedly, even if you knock him out (he will not be a true Karateka if he loses his temper). But when he is trying to help you, do not try to strike him unless he insists; it is not very pleasant to receive a blow, perhaps a damaging one, when one is in the process of explaining or correcting something.

Finally, in every Dojo there is an appointed Professor. You must NEVER call him "Master", as this is at one and the same time ironic in its implications, insulting (a "Master" is a man of accomplishment who has nothing more to learn; there are but one or two in a generation or a century), and it does him a disservice (in the beginning he will be confused, then he will find it rather agreeable, and finally he will take it for granted . . . and make no more progress). Always call him "Sensei". If the Professor has created a great number of other Professors you can express a deep respect by using the term "O-Sensei", but never "Master". Besides, are you quite sure that you are not putting your Professor on a pedestal in order to bask in his reflected glory?

The celebrated Karate Master Enri, who had studied Zen under the direction of an extremely severe teacher who went so far as to thrash his disciples (those who could not put up with it, left) used to say: "a disciple with limited understanding uses a Master's influence"; an intelligent disciple PROGRESSES WITH STRENGTH under a Master's direction. It is the same vis-a-vis a "Sensei".

If you do not completely understand the deep significance of these words, this will be normal. Consider Karate training as a test which you must pass, with perseverance, sincerity and thoroughness. As a passion which you are neither able nor willing to let pass you by.

If you keep at it, you will be able to affirm that many things in your everyday life have changed (studies, business affairs, family). You will not just have a new feeling about life (which is itself a battle) about genuine defence (fortunately rare) and HEALTH. It is strange to discover how few people think about preparing themselves for a long and healthy life, while refusing to even consider their own mortality. As if they had become possessed of permanent good health!

54

UDE-UKE

With the forearm you can block easily and powerfully any attack at stomach level, by a movement from the outside inwards (Soto-Uke, see below) or from the inside outwards (Uchi-Uke) as illustrated on the right. The two movements can follow each other in cases where the attacker uses a double attack (a blow with the fist or the right foot followed immediately by a blow with the left).

To perform SOTO-UKE, you start from the fighting posture in Zen-Kutsu (forward leg bent), and block by lowering the right arm (edge of the fist, forearm or elbow) quickly and strongly, while bringing the left fist back to the left hip. As in all the defences, the shoulders are turned sideways on. This is the only block in which the arms are not crossed.

To perform UCHI-UKE, which could be called more logically Ude-Uke, you cross your arms, turn the shoulders sideways on and block by striking from the inside outwards (either with the base of the thumb, or with the Kote, in the region of the wrist).

Ude-Uke is performed in Zen-Kutsu or in Ko-Kutsu and also with both hands, the left reinforcing the right. In attack, Ude-Uke can become Ura-Ken, but generally the Kiba-Dachi or Fudo-Dachi posture is preferable.

Ude-Uke (Blocking with the forearm).   Soto-Ude-Uke   Uchi-Ude-Uke

From the time that growth ceases, one begins to decline. Sclerosis of the eyes, for example, sets in at the age of twenty. At thirty, the troubles commence. But you still have more than double, perhaps three times this amount of active life ahead of you, in full possession of your faculties. Whatever "good reasons" you may have for interrupting your Karate (money, family, etc.) all will seem stupid, without importance, when you are bed-ridden, infirm and an invalid for 10, 20 or 40 years. Your physical health does not come from nature alone (too many things in modern life can destroy you) but from what you can do to conserve and develop it. There is no better physical or mental exercise than Karate. This is a certainty.

But, after all, this is your own problem.

Karate and Architecture

All the higher aspects of Karate meet again in all the Schools when one approaches near to perfection. I was surprised to find, when speaking with the old Masters in Japan, that they all had the same ideas and had no points of disagreement.

Each envisaged different situations and applications, such as defence against a normal individual, defence against a soldier trying to kill one, against several opponents, for championships, for the mental aspects, etc. . . . naturally enough, each was persuaded that he was nearest to the truth, as I am myself. I cannot see how one can spend a lifetime seeking mastery in a field in which one does not have confidence. It is necessary to have faith in what one does.

I can see no better way of helping you to understand than to compare the different Schools with the different forms of architectural conception in the World. Some constructed wooden huts, practically without foundations because this was sufficient to afford protection for a reasonable length of time; it was quick, and stood up well to average earth tremors: THIS IS THE EASY KARATE, quick to learn, valuable under normal circumstances, bestowing few mental and physical benefits. At the other extreme, we have those who built concrete blockhouses which can resist everything; wars, tempests, violent earthquakes; it takes a long time to build, it is without imagination, but unshakable: THIS IS THE KARATE OF FORCE, such as that of OKINAWA, not very attractive, difficult to master but in reality very dangerous. And we have the constructions of to-day. Those which are rapidly erected with prefabricated elements on light foundations, quickly excavated, nevertheless useful and sufficiently solid for modern life: THIS IS THE MODERN KARATE, with numerous styles pivoting above all on competition, in which one can envisage many varied techniques (in order to make it popular . . . and profitable, just like the prefabricated buildings). I think that you can now make your own comparisons between other forms of construction and other schools of KARATE. These majestic buildings which are based on foundations dug deep and for a long time, since one can see them rise upwards and upwards. Temples and Churches, etc. All the constructions have the same initial purpose: to protect Man against the elements, the vagaries of the weather, but with different means, degrees of durability and values.

One might suppose that everything has already been discovered and investigated about Karate, but one would be correct to doubt this . . . or to try to rediscover for yourself, as the great experts had a horror of leaving written advice. The true experience is that which you rediscover for yourself (that is why the real SENSEI is more a guide than a trainer or an Instructor.)

56

SHUTO-UKE

The "Edge of the Hand" (Shuto) is, by reason of its power, a particularly efficient defence (attacks with the edge of the hand are performed in the same way). It is relatively easy with a block to break the forearm or wrist of a person who has had no Karate training.

For Shuto-Uke you put yourself in Kokutsu-Dachi posture (Dachi, in a compound word, or TACHI at the beginning of a word: posture. KOKUTSU: weight of the body to the rear). The rear leg carries about 80 per cent of the body weight and the forward heel is slightly raised. In Ken-Kutsu, the front leg carries 50 per cent to 60 per cent of the body weight.

The finger tips must be directed towards the opponent's eyes and must never rise above the level of. the shoulders in all defences at middle range (the arm bent at an angle of 90 per cent, never extended).

As when attacking, you must never let your shoulders move while blocking. Stay with your hips at the same level when moving forwards or backwards during defences. Never let your eyes leave those of your opponent. If you do not concentrate your force (the muscles under the armpit are but the first step!) you will never be able to block or deflect a really strong attack.

Shuto-Uke (Blocks with the edge of the hand)

Soto-Shuto-Uke

Uchi-Shuto-Uke

Panorama—The Fundamental Principles of Karate

In order to be effective, the practice of Karate must take account of certain principles of which the most important are these: pure, raw, human energy (which can be real dynamite); concentration of physical and mental force (close union between the two); contraction (without which you will be very vulnerable); de-contraction (without which speed is impossible); reflexes (without which you will always be too late), and self-mastery in order to keep your mind clear (without which you merit nothing).

Energy

Every man, woman, and even every child, has an energy which is quite unsuspected and the power of which is truly astounding. This is proved by the fact that it needs eight men to hold down an epileptic in the course of an attack; four to restrain a crazed man, and every week the newspapers tell of incredible exploits under desperate situations (men or women caught in fires, on mountains, when their lives are in danger). This energy therefore really exists, because it can manifest itself in particular cases. We use only 30 per cent to 40 per cent of our energy daily, while having the feeling that we are using it all.

In fact, it is only in really desperate situations that we call on the maximum of our strength, by a complete liberation of our instinct of self-preservation which permits us to use 100 per cent of our energy. Ordinarily, we are mentally blocked by certain factors such as education, or civilization. This is why in KARATE one must continually call on the instinct of self-preservation during training, whence the axiom "kill or be killed". This state of mind is the shortest way to rapid progress.

Concentration

To liberate 100 per cent of your energy is a fine thing, yet it must not be squandered. It must be concentrated. For this, the traditional techniques are important (rear heel on the ground, strength in the advanced leg, hips low, etc.). One can say that the Karate techniques consist of concentrating the bodily energy in one single point, not just in blocking but also in attack. Needless to say, this concentration is physical: concentration of the muscles in one direction, speed, reaction, synchronization, and all together at the impact. But it is also mental, that is to say, psychic: the synchronization cannot be obtained without mental concentration on the object to be attained, but it requires a certain state of mind for too much mental concentration nullifies the perfect action of the body (the Zen aspect of KARATE).

Decontraction

This has many graduations in KARATE. Some muscles contract more slowly than others (due to the quality of the muscular fibres or the length of the fascicles), therefore when one decontracts, it is necessary to preserve a certain tone to the body in order to be able to act like a flash and in a single block, in a single action. This demands quite a long practice and mastery, and is exciting as well. Just as the mind which, in order to be active and quick, must be neither too contracted nor too decontracted, just attentive. If not, you will react very dangerously to the opponent's slightest feint. "Graduated" decontraction is indispensable if you are to be always ready to follow your adversary, to anticipate his attack (true Karate is defensive, but it is necessary to have reached an advanced level to understand it truly), to sense the right moment to attack or block, to follow up immediately with an effective counter-attack (to the right place and the right level).

SHUTO-BARAI

The "Sweep with the edge of the hand" or SHUTO-BARAI, is not well known or understood.

From the point of view of execution, it differs little from Shuto-Uke, but it is its application that is so interesting.

This block can be low or high, but at the same time it is followed by a sweeping action to the side in order to hold and to unbalance (laterally forward or laterally to the rear) as can be seen opposite.

In the pure Jodan-Shuto-Uke, the elbow should be rather higher than in the illustrations, it should be at shoulder level. The other hand should preferably be at the side, fist closed in the classic hikite position, or open in front of the stomach as in the classic shuto position.

When Shuto-Barai is performed at middle level, the sweeping hand can have the wrist bent (this can facilitate the action in certain cases) instead of being perfectly straight and in line with the forearm as in the classic Shuto-Uke.

The practise of Jodan-Shuto-Uke is excellent for strengthening the costal and dorsal regions, which should be tensed even while the arm is raised.

Soto-Shuto-Uke   Uchi-Shuto-Uke

Jodan Shuto-Barai (Sweeping with the edge of the hand)

Contraction

If decontraction is very difficult because of its demand for great modifications (stomach always strong, buttocks likewise, etc.) contraction is equally very difficult. So difficult in fact that many schools get around the problem in the simplest way by cutting out the necessary training.

A good karateka should have protective muscles like armour plating. It is distressing to see combatants in competition gasping for breath at the slightest uncontrolled blow with the fist or foot (in competition, one should in theory stop the blow at skin level). I can imagine the grimace of displeasure with which the old Karate men of Japan would view this. At black-belt level one should be able to take any blow with fist or foot on any part of the body, except of course, on the lower abdomen, the nose or the eyes. This holds true if you remain immobile (and do not become vulnerable as when you advance into certain good attacks).

It is for this reason that in true Karate one tries to strike the opponent when he is advancing towards you, thereby doubling the strength of your attack by his forward movement (he impales himself). The Goju-Ryu school, which perhaps insists a little too much on this aspect of contraction, is in the right for many forms and styles of speed make one wonder what would happen in the case of combat against several opponents if they cannot stand up against exceptional attacks.

Together with contraction, one should study the manner of deep breathing without which the full energy cannot be attained, and which can in itself render certain attacks harmless (particularly to the solar plexus by a special position of the diaphragm).

Reflexes

A reflex is an unconscious nervous reaction to a sensory perception which makes you act in a certain way. From birth we have acquired a great many reflexes. Even a baby makes an attempt at a defensive reflex action when one gives it a smack. The gestures of KARATE are all natural reflexes of defence, they are "pure reflexes", therefore, slightly deviated or improved for the sake of a greater efficiency. This is the very important difference to the gestures of Judo or Aikido, which are gestures of technique, the products of thought, seen through the intelligence, acquired reflexes (as pulling when one is pushed; this has a perfect efficacy, but it is against nature. Otherwise one would be falling over all the time when going down the street, in the underground, or elsewhere). Also, one loses practically all efficiency when one ceases to practise these sports, though one can keep the reflexes acquired in KARATE indefinitely after having reached a certain level, even after training has ceased, just as one can still swim after twenty or more years without having done any swimming, once a certain degree of ability has been reached.

Blocks and counter-attacks must become automatic and one single action. A spectator should see the two actions as one, indivisible movement.

Self-Mastery

After all that I have been able to say about the fundamental principles of KARATE, it is clear that the mental aspect is just as important as the physical (if not more so) for the attainment of mastery. Note that I say "mastery" and not mastery of Karate, for once you have gained the latter you will automatically gain all the other masteries on a level above the normal.

You must have noticed that in an earlier chapter I said that KARATE was defensive. If all

AGE-UKE

These photographs show the Jodan-Age-Uke, that is to say, the way to defend oneself (Uke) with the forearm by blocking a high attack (Jodan). It is a very strong defence against all high attacks, whether with the fist, foot, a stick, or anything else and also against holds. At the end of the block the nails must be turned towards the opponent so as to present the fleshy part of the arm to the attack (if you were to turn your nails towards your head, your forearm would be broken in certain very strong attacks).

Note the concentration of force in the groin, and the lowered shoulder. It is impossible to turn aside a strong attack if the shoulder is raised. Another fault to avoid, one that is common to many Karate men, even the Japanese, lies in the position of the shoulders. They must be three-quarters on in defence and square on in attack. If the shoulders are square on in defence, a violent attack has every chance of touch- a vital spot. The experts turn their shoulders even more, almost to the point where they are sideways on, without hindering the speed of the right-hand counter-attack.

Soto-Age-Uke   Uchi-Age-Uke

Jodan Age-Uke (Rising block)

the Katas in Karate begin with a defence, there are many reasons. One of them is that the basis of KARATE is self-control. It is obvious that if you keep your composure, the attack becomes unthinkable. Only the stupidity of war could justify it. In all other cases, even when life is in danger, defensive KARATE is preferable. Because defence begins while the opponent is attacking, and the attack can be at the intuitive stage, that is to say at the precise instant when something cracks in his mind and he decides to strike, defence and attack can appear to be a single action to the uninitiated observer.

The time to think about defence is not when the killer's revolver bullets have struck home, nor when he squeezes the trigger, nor when he has put his hand in his pocket. It is as he is about to put his hand in his pocket that one should defend oneself according to the spirit of Karate. This attack is therefore essentially defensive. I am not putting this precisely just to justify your action, but to guide you on "the true way of the true KARATE". For this, you need a great mastery over your own self, a serenity even, which alone will enable you to gauge his intentions. Though fear and anger can perhaps generate energy, they do so at the expense of lucidity, precision and concentration. This can only come as the result of long training, principally in KATAS and KUMITES of the conventional type (Ten-no-Kata and Sanbon-Kumites).

Total Efficacy

It is evident that if one attains this mastery one becomes a veritable superman, from all points of view. Unfortunately, a man is just a man, with all his weaknesses and imperfections (to a greater or lesser degree). And besides, even if one attains this mastery at odd moments, it is very difficult to maintain it in a stable way. This is why those who are touched by this mastery, "illuminated" by the human possibilities, pursue their KARATE training to the day they die. But how can one speak about this aspect which is such a special one. It is not peculiarly the illumination of ZEN or SATORI, neither is it in any way supra-normal. It is simply a quite astonishing perception of what the mind and body can achieve in moments of complete lucidity and total liberty.

These searchings after total efficacy are rendered indispensable by the fact that one prepares oneself every day in KARATE for desperate situations. For example, the fight against several opponents (as in the Katas, which are instructional dramas). In such a case, a single blow should be decisive. Whether it is a block (which is equally a blow and an unbalancing action), it is necessary that the result should be reached in a single movement.

Just One Chance!

All training pivots on this end, understandably difficult to achieve in practice though it is because the opponent is also filled with the instincts of defence and preservation; he moves out of the way, he is ready for you. In spite of all this, it is necessary to succeed. The ideal is to strike a vital spot by means of ATEMI (there are many in the body). But the true KARATE should eventually be so effective that the result would be absolute and immediate, no matter how small the area that is struck. This is what happens in practice when one has obtained a certain sensation called "KIME", and which is very difficult to translate into Western languages. At this stage every attack or counter-attack gives an immediate result.

Are you tempted by the possibilities of KARATE?

The way (Do) will be hard, full of aches, pains, and sometimes, tears, yet with far fewer blows and injuries than you might suppose (there are very few accidents compared with Judo, for

UCHI-KOMI

The "Close-quarters Block", or Uchi-Komi is typical of Master Funakoshi's teaching.

It is frequently confused with Ude-Uke (Soto-Ude-Uke) and yet the difference is equally important as between a block (such as Shuto-Uke) and a sweep (Shuto-Barai).

The idea is that a block effected strongly and correctly will halt an opponent's advance. It follows therefore that one counter-attacks a man who is immobile. But if one blocks with a sweeping action, the opponent's body continues to advance and your counter-attack is thereby doubled in effect. It is therefore better to close-in. This technique is much more difficult, and this is why it is found at the end of the Ten-no Kata from which we have just described the six blocks.

It is useless to raise the fist before performing Uchi-Komi (a warning useful for a block, but useless for a sweep). Instead, one must perform a sweeping block just preceding the rear shoulder (following the opponent's advance, to a small extent if he stops as in Fig. 3 of the disengagement, or more in the other examples shown opposite).

To avoid all confusion, name all the blocks from the interior towards the exterior (in relation to your body). Ude-Uke, and Uchi-Komi for all blocks from the exterior towards the interior of your body. The first word, "Soto" or "Uchi", shows whether you block the opponent's arm outwards or inwards: Soto-Uchi-Komi, Uchi-Uchi-Komi, Soto-Ude-Uke, Uchi-Ude-Uke (or if you prefer, Soto-Soto-Uke, Uchi-Soto-Uke, Soto-Uchi-Uke, Uchi-Uchi-Uke).

Soto-Uchi-Komi   Uchi-Uchi-Komi

Uchi-Komi (Close quarters block)

example, which is in the second rank of sports from the aspect of accident insurance). On the other hand, you must clench your teeth and hold on, this will be a test and a much greater one than ever imagined. At any rate, it will be if your Professor (whom you should call SENSEI and never Master) is up to his job. For the spirit cannot be mastered without severe tests, like electric shocks. These tests are designed to enable you to perceive your true possibilities and to bring you to what is like a new birth. But the result justifies the hardship. And after all, it is so much the better if many things are renounced . . . in this way, we "poor average men" can surpass the rest for the benefits resulting from KARATE influence family and social life every day. This is evident.

The Kumites all derive from the Ten-no-Kata, which is the ideal Kata and the most instructive for rapid progress in efficacy and in spirit.

You will certainly have heard mention of KARATE-DO, in a rather pejorative sense as opposed to KARATE. KARA means "empty", TE "hand", and DO means "way". KARATE is therefore the art of combat with the bare hands, and KARATE-DO is the "way through the art of combat with the bare hands". To me, these both mean the same thing, but those who use the term KARATE-DO want to say that they are seeking above all the mental benefits, the way, of KARATE. This is nonsense, for one cannot progress in one without the other, not physically without removing the mental blocks, not mentally without "pulverising" the body. Also, the great majority of serious practitioners say simply KARATE. The greatest difficulty this art is to be modest, e.g., with a just evaluation of one's own weaknesses and one's own worth. Perhaps you are curious about the significance of the words. Here then is the true sense of "KARA" and "DO". "KARA" or "empty" signifies not merely the absence of arms, but also of evil intentions, a pure mind, a non-mental state.

What Is "Do"

What is then this word "DO" with which it has been the fashion since the end of the Middle Ages in Japan (around 1900) to add not only to all the Martial Arts, but also to flower arrangement, ceremonies (tea, dancing, games, chess, etc.)?

It is the "Way", the unification of body and mind towards a more completely co-ordinated action. It is this "Way" which is sought by the Yogis of India, the Ascetics, the religious and the philosophers. It is rather like this "Way" when you toss a stone and it lands on the chosen target without previous thought on your part. Astounded by your skill, you try to do it again . . . and the stone falls a foot short: too much mental concentration.

The second time, your body was restrained by your mind and the two were united when you did it first of all, because you had a complete detachment regarding the result. This is a very important aspect of KARATE which one finds again in Japanese fencing, and which is impossible to describe in so few lines. Nevertheless, perhaps you have understood this "DO" without which it is absolutely impossible to parry a genuine attack or to attack yourself. Also, that the exact meaning of KARATE-DO is "ATTAINMENT OF THE WAY THROUGH KARATE". This is why KARATE is at once a terrible weapon, a physical culture and a mental education. It is also the most "balanced" of all sports because the actions of all KATAS are executed on both sides, and in the KUMITES one must become adept on both the right and the left, in front and behind, and in which one exercises all the limbs in all directions, in contraction as well as in extension.

I should also like to assert that KARATE is not a static study of attack and defence movements, but is on the contrary a genuine sport. A sport which has been perfected for 3,000 years, mostly on the field of battle. To imagine what is represented by 30 centuries of technical progress, think of the evolution realised in just half a century of boxing, where the Champions who originated the modern style are still living.

64

Karate for All Ages—But Different

As I have told you, there are many styles of KARATE. I do not wish to speak of the forms which seek maximum efficacy by means of combat (real against several or in Championships against one opponent) but of their diverse manners of training.

Children, then, from six to twelve years of age can, together with women, practise Karate without difficulty. The training is of course centred on exercise in space and on the supple Katas.

At the age of strength and vigour, one can practise training in pairs (KUMITES=hand to hand=assaults) with five steps, three steps, or one step (Gohon-Kumite, Sanbon-Kumite, Ippon-Kumite).

As far as the level of progress permits, the Katas (conventional combat in space against six or eight imaginary opponents) can become possible at fighting speed, as can the free combats and the referred competitions. These are the virile tests which can be pursued up to around thirty years of age.

After 30 to 35 years, one should enter into KARATE with real blows, man to man, according to the degree of proficiency and other conditions. At this stage, to be true to your self means that you must hit as fast and as hard as possible, this is what your opponent expects. It is a stage at which one acquires exceptional mental benefits, but one which many people avoid.

After 40-45 years, one concentrates on mental research, the mastery of Body-Spirit (Ying-Yang). KARATE is one of the very rare Martial Arts which one can pursue alone (continuing to make real progress regardless of age).

Examples of
Ippon-Kumite
(single attack)

Developments

How to Walk and Turn in Karate

The manner of walking, peculiar to KARATE, is extremely important. It is true to say that every detail in KARATE is "extremely important" and that nothing can be neglected.

It is a characteristic that when one advances or retreats, the knees are pressed together in the middle of the step (photographs on page 67) in order to protect the lower abdomen (among other reasons) and without relaxing the knees. That is to say, the belt and the head always remain at the same level as one progresses. The distance between the feet can be reduced, and for extra speed one can merely slide one knee past the other without worrying too much about defence, which is instinctive in cases of need.

The feet should brush the ground (without dragging as in Judo), not slapping or "challenging" (as in French boxing), lightly and strongly but without raising the heel (nor dancing on the balls of the feet as in English boxing). In certain rare cases and only at an advanced technical level, these "faults" can be utilized, but we are now entering into strategy and special cases reserved for black-belts of 2nd Dan and over.

66

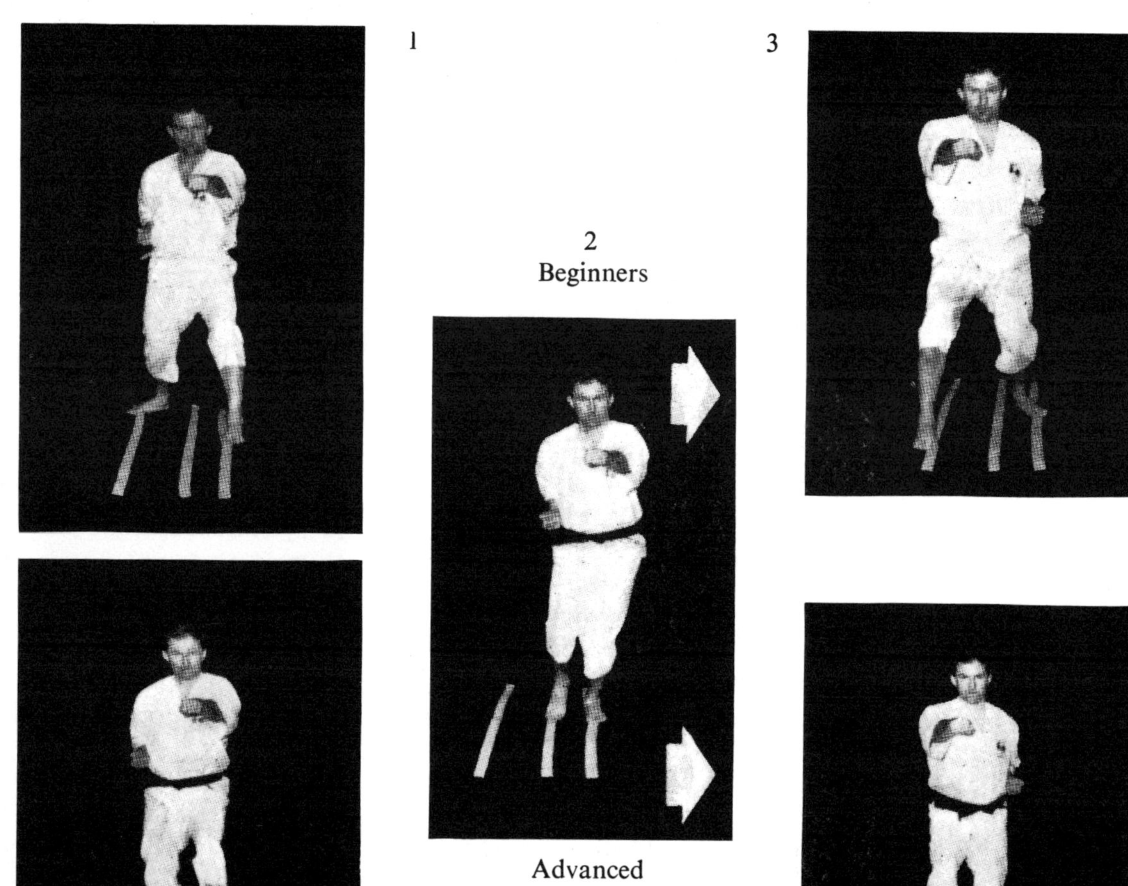

Developments in Zen-Kutsu

You should not move forward by shifting the balance of the body as in normal walking, but by "pulling" on the knee of the advanced leg which then comes vertically over the big toe (Fig. 1 and 1a). The difficulty is to bring back the rear leg very quickly without bending, swaying or jerking the upper body or the arms. For this, put your strength between your legs and think "forwards, faster and faster still" by doing the Kihon (exercises which one performs in space without a partner—at the beginning of the session after loosening-up exercises—to warm yourself and to acquire strength, speed and relaxation).

Place strength in the soles of your feet more than in your toes, the edges of your feet (little toe side) and your heels. Do not tap with either the front or the back foot. Your advance must be as quick as light without the slightest preliminary sign. Do not move the advanced foot at the beginning of the step (a serious fault with beginners is to turn the toes of the advanced foot outwards before stepping forward).

To move forward is of course important, but to move backwards is not less so. Practise moving backwards quickly as seriously as moving forwards quickly, always keeping your body as low as possible and without raising the heels.

Past 55-60 years, one practises KARATE for health. And KARATE is so effective in preserving health, for quickening or relaxing tension, for maintaining nervous activity, the good functioning of the organs, and above all mental health, that in China it was practised with no other object in view. It happens very often that KARATE is prescribed by a doctor in the case of an elderly man or woman to bring back suppleness and muscular tone, to combat anxiety or a psychic derangement. This KARATE is naturally very slow, combining suppleness with contraction according to the end being sought, and it then becomes a genuine therapy. It is practically ignored by most people in the West and this is a great pity, for we have nothing like it in the Occident. It is a sort of active Yoga, having also the same manner of respiration.

The photographs on page 67 show how, as one progresses, one can reduce the distance between the feet. On page 69 we show you how to pivot.

To Advance or Retreat in Combat?
To advance on the attack is the beginning and end of Karate. It is the one way which can ensure that the opponent is put out of action with the maximum of certainty. It demands courage and technique but it is the most rewarding in real combat and the richest in mental benefits in training. It is the one way which can give a small man the chance to defeat a big and strong one. This is why height, weight and strength need not, so to speak, be taken into account in Karate. Much less than in ANY OTHER SPORT Western or Oriental. We shall explain why.

Imagine that you possess a power of five units and that a man twice as strong as you, that is with ten units, has decided to kill you with a blow of his right fist. The fist can be empty, armed with a knife, razor, broken bottle, etc. the attack is the same and the fact is this: this fist will kill you if it touches you. You have three possibilities while he is advancing to strike: (1) retreat—(2) advance—(3) evade.

(1) Retreat: this is the most natural reaction. If the aggressor is courageous, as you must always presume him to be, he will pursue you and strike with the other fist or the foot, if not with the same hand. You will be lost. If, having retreated, you can nevertheless counter-attack, you hit him with all your force, but five units against ten units will not put him out of action. In any case, it is uncertain, even though some vital points are very delicate (the eyes are an example which can be the most easily understood).

(2) Advance: If while advancing you can manage to brush past the attack or turn it aside, a fraction of an inch is sufficient and this would be best. In a fight to the death, give your cheek, ear or even your eye if this will enable you to save your life by putting the aggressor out of action WITH CERTAINTY. Your counter-attack of five units will be added to ten units of the attacker as he advances . . . and the impact will have a force of 15 units, or very nearly. Even a child can break the bones of a giant in this way if, of course, his own bones are more resistant (his elbow or head against the sides, or the collar-bone of someone stronger, etc.).

Half-turn on one spot (in Kihon)

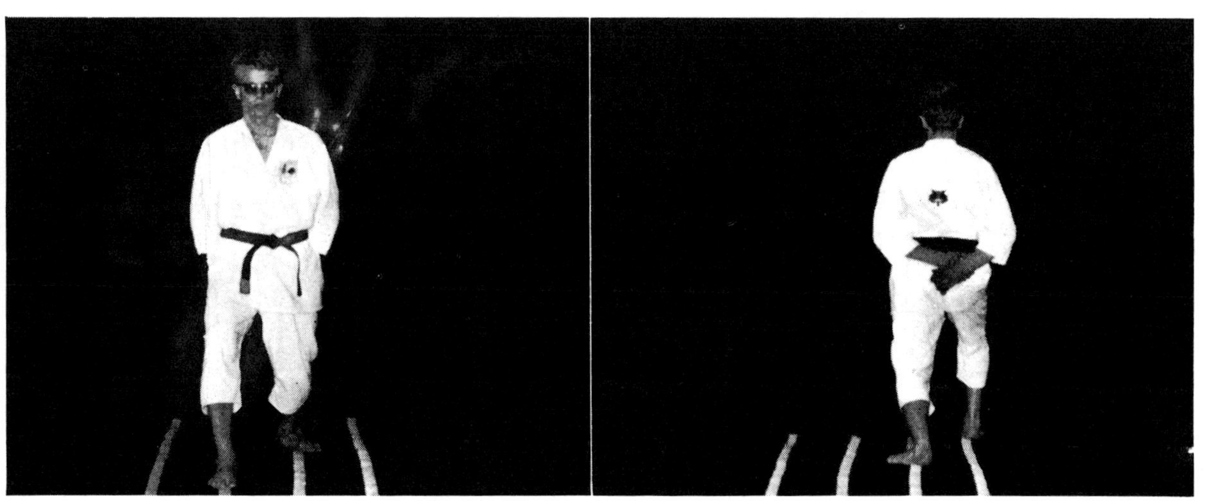

Half-turn while advancing (in Katas)

Retreat-Advance
in Ko-Kutsu
(all grades)

(3) Evade: A sideways movement, for example, is an excellent way to avoid being struck but it gives the minimum of possibilities for putting the aggressor out of action with a single counter-attack.

Your body being sideways on, your upper body laterally inclined, your counter-attack will have the force only of your shoulder or your leg. Probably insufficient for a decisive result unless one is already an expert, in which case one can use other techniques (thrust to the eyes, circular kick, sweeping, etc.).

The beginner should always try to advance on the attack. Once the attack has been mastered, by "strategy" or sometimes with a blow, he will be able to retreat, evade, feint, etc. things which are DETRIMENTAL BEFORE KARATE 1st DAN.

To advance on the attack demands the greatest concentration, moderation of movement, the fastest changes of position, controlled breathing, strength centred in the lower abdomen (tanden), the Kiai, the martial look (attentive, not revealing your intentions, eyelids steady, etc.) and the feeling of hand-to-hand combat. Courage develops, fear disappears and gives place to a great clarity. The necessity of using basic techniques in the most rigorous way so as not to be in danger makes one see many other aspects.

For the same reason, a beginner, that is to say below black-belt (which is the BEGINNING of mastery and not the end) should concentrate on single attacks. ONE SINGLE attack, with all the energy and knowledge possible: "if it fails, it is death". After 1st Dan, combinations and feints are, of course, interesting. But let us note that from 2nd Dan, the Karateka strive like the great experts to return to the single attack, for the straight line is the most sure.

In the same way, the question of the use of leg or hand. Under black belt, the beginner has the feeling of being safer with attacks or counter-attacks with the leg. At black-belt, one becomes conscious of the use of the hands, at the same time as the feet. But one quickly discovers that the foot is only relatively efficient. The great expert uses the hand more than the foot, just as the artillery opens the way for the attack but rarely carries off the victory alone because it is necessary to occupy the terrain.

The Karateka must, of course, always think of improving his technique so as not to rely on his youthful vitality which will disappear in time. If he spends too long on Ju-Kumite and neglects the Katas and the Ki-hon it is evident that he will develop bad habits which will hold back his progress. It is necessary just to perform Kumite in order to train the "Ki" and to augment the Kumite with Katas, Sanbon and Ippon Kumite as his experience grows.

3. Competition
Karate is comprised of several forms of competition. Free Fighting or Ju-Kumite which, as the name implies, is a form of combat aimed at the acquiring of technique and variety. Refereed Fighting which can be displayed in the DOJO or in public (Championship) dates from the post-war years. The Fight against Several Opponents, which is already difficult in itself, becomes a real problem because one cannot strike one's partners in the DOJO in the same way as one would in genuine combat.

70

Free fighting is essential, even for beginners (for short periods), in order not to lose the spontaneous sense of combat,the "KI" (spirit), to discover all the modifications of application (Sen, Sen-no-Sen, Gonosen, etc.). Knowledge of the techniques, their execution according to the standard forms, with strength and speed, is still not KARATE . . . if one cannot apply them with the spontaneity and feeling of free combat.

This is why the Championships, decried by some and appreciated by others, is important. In the same way as the SHIWARI (Breaking Tests) it is a test of efficacy, a trial, a control. It is true that the Championship does not express the "total fight for survival in the gravest situation" which one likes to imagine was the true KARATE of ancient times (against several opponents on the battlefield). But it also is true that those who do not participate in Championships will know nothing of their possibilities against a single man, will never be able to face several.

It must be understood that one loses half, if not three-quarters of one's power in championship, as in real combat. If one trains with the hips very low, one will be almost upright in a championship. If one trains with the hips high, one will be weak and vulnerable in serious combat.
Moreover, all those who take part in Championships become sincere, honest and courageous men, though one finds those who take advantage of their strength against weaker men, liars, thieves and perjurers among those who do not take part (or who do not take part any more even when they have the opportunity, as I have confirmed in the course of several distressing affairs). This is a necessary test which must be faced.

For myself, I know that I would never have found, rediscovered I should say, certain important secrets of KARATE which I have in part confided to you if I had not carried out many combats . . . including the challenges which I had to face since I first launched KARATE in Europe, and which led to richly instructive experiences. These things are solely for my personal gratification, because publicity is my profession.

Shiai

This is the refereed competition. It can take place in the Dojo (grading examinations at the end of the month, Tsukinami Shiai) or in public (championship). It is different to Ju-Kumite in that defeats are counted and are decided by the referee, who is in a better position to judge than yourself. One does not always understand the realities. This is why the championship is essential. One can even say that when the attacks are really effective, one does not understand at all. As in boxing, those who have been knocked out are nearly always astonished on waking up and wonder what has happened to them. To take part in a championship is often very deceptive, but always very profitable. There also, one must not actually land a blow nor cause injury, otherwise one loses the contest through lack of control.

All the Kumites are intended to produce instantaneous counter-attacking reflexes. Blocking, dodging and defending yourself are instinctive (well or badly, you are continually making sketchy defensive gestures from the day you draw your first breath). But the counter-attack is always very slow to come (mental blocks). Therefore, it is necessary to try to block and counter-attack (so as to get in the first blow) . . . this demands much practice and mental mastery.

Ju-Kumite and Beginners

Contrary to what one might think, experience has proved that it is a good thing to perform Kumite (even Ju-Kumite) from the very beginning in Karate. For the fighting instinct, the "Ki", which is something like "punch", "vitality", is present in all of us to a greater or lesser degree and can be developed without limit, but it can be easily lost. Too much exercising without mental application can emasculate a beginner in Karate who would have been able to become exceptional. But up to brown belt one should not exceed five minutes of Kumite in training. Then the beginner will find his favourite attack, which he will continue to perfect for the rest of his life, and through which he will sense the truth of other attacks. Karate is combat, which one must improve in efficiency. It must never under any circumstances become a dance without spirit, even an elegant one. The precise role of the "Sensei" is to guide his pupils towards a greater efficiency through training. It is no solution to cover up the difficulties.

Rules of Competition

The time of the combats shall be fixed prior to the competition. When the time has elapsed, the referee and the contestants shall be informed by a clear signal or by voice. A decision must be rendered obligatorily.

At the start, the contestants salute each other at a distance of three metres apart, in the centre of the competition area, and the contest shall not commence until the call of "HAJIME" by the referee (the ceremonial kneeling bow of Karate can take the place of the standing salutation, according to a decision made before the competition). At the end of the contest, the contestants shall return to their original position and, feet together, wait until the referee tells them to bow. The result of the contest will be announced before the final salute.

The officials shall be composed of:

—A competition Director who shall be in a position where he can see the whole contest area clearly. His rôle will be to organise and supervise the competitions.

—A directing contest referee who shall ensure accordance with the rules and announce the results. The referee shall have the sole responsibility for the conduct of the contest. A co-referee may be designated who would circle the contestants together with the referee.

—Two or four judges shall be posted at the corners of the competition area. They shall note, each on his own behalf, their impressions and indicate the contestant they consider to be the winner by a red or white signal when requested to do so by the referee. They shall signal an excess of the limit during the contest, and which has not been noticed by the referee, by raising their coloured signal, but without intervening in any other way either by voice or gesture.

After the time limit, and if there has not been a definite victory (ippon), the referee shall consult the official judges and give the decision of the majority. Only the following terms shall be used: the start of the contest: hajime (begin), a break: ayame or break, the end of the contest: yasume (enough).

Official Terms used by the Referee

HAJIME—Begin.

IPPON—Point.

WAZA-ARI—Advantage ($\frac{1}{2}$ point).

WAZA-ARI AWASETE IPPON—Two waza-aris making one full point.

BREAK—the contestants release each other.

YOSHI—the contest continues.

STOP.

HANTEI—Decision.

HIKI-WAKE—Draw.

TIME.

FUSEN-SHO—Violation of the rules.

YUSEI-GACHI—Victory by superiority.

MAITTA—Indication of surrender (I am beaten).

HANSOKU-MAKE—Loss through violation of the rules (disqualification).

Gestures Used by the Referee

IPPON—The right hand extended forwards at an angle of 30 per cent from the vertical.

WAZA-ARI—The right hand extended horizontally to the side.

HANTEI—The right hand extended vertically upwards.

HIKI-WAKE—The two hands crossed on the body then separated.

The Competition Area

Karate competitions shall take place in an area measuring at least eight metres along one side and not exceeding ten metres, with the limits clearly indicated in white or red. The surface shall be flat, smooth, made of polished or painted boards, tatami or tarpaulin according to what is available, but of wood for preference.

The Contestants' Equipment

The contestants shall wear a Karategi of white, or sometimes black. By karategi one means the clothing commonly called a "kimono" in the West, and which consists of:

—A jacket with sleeves covering the elbows, but less than half way down the forearms.

—Trousers of the same colour reaching below the middle of the lower legs.

—A belt long enough to go twice around the body and which is tied correctly with a flat knot at the level of the waist, and which shall have the loose ends at least 15 cm. and not exceeding 20 cm. in length. The colour varies according to the grade and there shall be a visible red line along its length.

The jackets can carry club insignia (Mon) without ostentation and without initials exceeding 2cm. in height. The Karategi shall be kept freshly ironed, with no tears or loose stitches.

The contestants will wear a protective box of a resistant material approved by the Federal Technical Commission.

Protection for the shins, forearms, knees, and elbows, and bandages whether adhesive or not are forbidden except in case of genuine injury on medical advice.

The contestants shall not wear any jewellery, or any metallic object liable to cause injury. Only wedding rings, if they have no sharp edges, may be tolerated if the contestants find themselves unable to remove them.

NOTE—Regarding the differences in relation to the clothing worn by Judoka, that worn by the Karateka is made of a crisper material which permits the "crack", the sign of a good attack. Also, it is not desirable that it should be held in place by two or four tapes as it tears easily.

Competition Rules (conclusion)

Signs of Defeat and Surrender

A contestant who considers himself beaten, injured, and unable to fight on or to resist any longer, can indicate his defeat by raising an arm in a sign of surrender. If he cannot raise an arm, he gives the signal of defeat by tapping two or more times with his hand or foot on his opponent's body or on the ground.

Vital points:
The vital points can be considered as: the face, neck, lower abdomen (private parts), solar plexus and the opponent's back.

Forfeiture:
A contestant who is not ready for combat immediately his name is called shall be declared "forfeit" and his opponent "winner by default" (Fusen-sho), whether it is due to inattention, absence, injury or any other reason.

No separation is made between contestants in terms of height, reach, strength or weight with the object of avoiding injuries, since the contestants do not strike each other in earnest on the vital points.

All cases not covered by the present regulations shall be considered by the official judges.

Grounds for Disqualification
—When a contestant does not immediately obey the instructions of the referee.
—When he loses his self-control to the point of putting his opponent in danger and of disregarding the prohibited acts.
—When he loses his sense of sportsmanship, gives voice to an opinion or protests against a decision of the referee or the judges.
—When his attitude can give rise to prejudice against the popularity and the spirit of Karate.

The referee can disqualify immediately without warning in what he considers to be grave cases. He can content himself with a warning, with an immediate stop to the contest, in cases where one or both the contestants attempt, or actually commit an infraction of the rules. A second warning brings disqualification.

In case of injuries

If an injury occurs in the course of a contest, and which prevents it being continued, the decision by the judges shall, after interruption by the referee, be made according to the following rules:
—If the injured contestant is responsible for his own injury, he loses if he cannot continue;
—If the injury is caused by the opponent, the injured man wins;
—If the cause of the injury cannot be determined, the injured man loses by surrender.

74

Strictly Prohibited Acts

—To actually strike the opponent's vital points in any manner. Even to touch them lightly is forbidden.

The stopping blows must be effected with controlled force against areas without vital points.

—To attack, or to simulate an attack, with the finger-tips towards the eyes and the hand open and extended.

—To actually bite or scratch. To take hold of the Karategi between the teeth.

—To hold, hang on to, or to prevent the opponent from moving without any immediate further action, that is to say, without necessity; standing: one second maximum; on the ground: three seconds maximum.

—To execute an attack liable to injure an opponent.

To turn one's back on the opponent. In evasions and rapidly turning combinations, every attack aimed at the back by an opponent can be counted as a "chi-mei" (mortal attack) by the referee if they show the possibility of power.

If the contestant remains with his back turned, even a light attack will be counted as "ippon".

—To avoid sincere combat with one's partner in any way, for example, with the evident object of waiting for the end of the time limit and the audible signal.

—All acts of disrespect towards an opponent, even with the tactical object of making him lose his self-control.

—To untie and re-tie the belt, the tapes of the Karategi or the trousers without having been asked to by the referee.

—It is formally forbidden for the contestants to speak.

You should avoid being drawn into taking up one particular style. In Karate, since the "International Karate Federation", separated from, but aided by the "International Judo Federation" have produced competition rules applicable to all styles, one should no longer speak of Schools (Ryu) but of Karate.

Example of Ippon-Kumite:
1. High block, followed by extension of the arm
   (as in certain Katas).

2. Sweep with a combined unbalancing action
   with hand and knee, followed by a counter-
   attack to the solar plexus.

THE GRADES

The Keikogi

The "kimono", but one calls it Keikogi or Karategi in Japan (clothing: "Gi", training: "Keiko") is not the same as in Judo. It is shorter, reaching just over the buttocks (in Kendo there are two small cords at the lower extremity, in Judo and Karate there are none). The sleeves are shorter. The material, this is very important, is less heavy and crisper: if attacks in space are good ones, the material "cracks" and serves as a criterion to beginners, in particular for blows with the fist and the edge of the band. The belt, shorter than in Judo, is tied low on the waist (and not on the hips as in Judo) in the traditional manner. This costume gives a Karate style at the first glance, and in this way one can easily distinguish the former Judo men from the Karateka who have never practised Judo. To the question which is often asked on this subject, it appears from the statistics that in Karate circles about 20 per cent are former Judoka, the remaining 80 per cent is comprised of 70 per cent men who have never practised another combat sport, and 10 per cent of boxers in the English or French styles.

Colours of the Grades

To permit a progression in training, and also as encouragement, there are grades in Karate as in nearly all the other Japanese sports. (In Japan there are Dan grades even for swimming and most of the other games and activities, for chess, flower arrangement, etc.). With us, categories and classes are equally frequent. The first grade is the "1st Dan" (Dan=step), and its possessor wears a black belt with a red thread (a black belt indicates the Dan grade in all Japanese sports). Below 1st Dan are the beginners, or Kyu (=class), who wear a white belt with a red thread from 9th to 6th Kyu inclusive, and a coloured belt with a red thread from 5th to 1st Kyu (some use the same colours as in Western Judo, white from 9th to 6th Kyu, yellow, orange, green, blue, brown from 5th to 1st Kyu but with a red thread). Among the Dan grades, the 5th Dan is the highest which has been awarded by the Master Funakoshi Certain Japanese schools have decided to award 10th Dan.

Table of Grades

Grades	Practise Times	Colour of the Belt
5th Dan	(10 to 20 years) (exceptional)	Expert Red or Black
4th Dan	(5 to 10 years)	Black—Red thread 4 bars
3rd Dan	(4 to 7 years)	Black—Red thread 3 bars
2nd Dan	(2 to 3 years)	Black—Red thread 2 bars
1st Dan	(1 to 2 years)	Black—Red thread
1st Kyu	(6 months)	Brown—Red thread
2nd Kyu	(6 months)	Blue—Red thread
3rd Kyu	(3 to 6 months)	Green—Red thread
4th Kyu	(2 months)	Orange—Red thread
5th Kyu	(2 months)	Yellow—Red thread
6th Kyu	(1 month)	White—Red thread 3 small bars
7th Kyu	(1 month)	White—Red thread 2 small bars
8th Kyu	(1 month)	White—Red thread 1 small bar
9th Kyu	(beginner)	White—Red thread Beginner

This table gives the average time required for a man of between 18 and 20 years of age, with two to three training sessions a week of an hour and a half. It will vary according to age and ability. The bases for the above are those of the principal Western and Japanese Dojos.

Numerous schools have chosen other colours (Violets, Purples, etc).

For 1st Dan

Before the examination, each candidate shall have fulfilled the following conditions:

—Be presented by his Professor (who will sign the competition card).

—Be in possession of an up-to-date federal licence (Karate section).

—Be of 1st Kyu (brown belt) grade.

—Have a minimum of two years of practise, certified by two successive licences

—Have his "competition card".

The examination is in two parts:

—Competition test (or pre-selection).

—Technical test.

PROGRAMME

First appearance of intuition and good anticipation. Mastery of the techniques and the former + the antique Katas. (Note: This table of grades is based on a gradation with 5th Dan as the maximum).

First appearance of the ability to anticipate blocks, sweeps and evasions. Impossible to carry out Gohon-Kumite and Sanbon-Kumite with 4th Dan, everything is reduced to Ippon-Kumite. Katas with personal interpretation.

Perfect mastery of the blocks (strong, sweeping) and evasions, direct counters in Ten-no-Kata to real blows from the natural and combat postures. Mastery of the former Katas. Remarkable results in competition.

Perfect mastery of the blocks (sweeping) and counter-attacks while advancing. Ippon-Kumites and Sanbon-Kumites at three levels (feet included). Former Katas + Tekki 2 and 3, Saipa, etc. . . . higher Katas.

Perfect mastery of the blocks (strong) and counter-attacks on the spot. Combination of competitive techniques in Ippon-Kumite (real ones). Mastery of the former Katas and Tekki, Passai, Kanku at combat speed + Sanchin.

Perfect execution of the five Eian (at combat speed) or Pinan (one for one). Knowledge of all the Karate techniques (and their Japanese names). Training directed towards competition. Katas, Tekki, Passai, Kanku.

Technical study of the five first Katas of Eian or Pinan, and execution at combat speed of Eian. Competition training. Combination of movements in Kihon.

Technical study of the four first Katas of Eian or Pinan. Ten-no-Kata from the combat posture. Ju-Kumite (free).
Katas = Eian or Pinan Yodan Shihozuki III—IV—VI.

Technical study of the three first Katas of Eian or Pinan. Yakusoku-Kumite and Sanbon-Kumite (three attacks).
Katas = Eian or Pinan Sandan—Shohozuki one and two.

All the basic and counter attack postures, Gohon-Kumite.
Katas = Ten-no-Kata—Eian or Pinan Nidan.

Middle level blocks (Uchikomi and Soto-Uke). Mawashi-Geri (circular kick).
Katas = Taikyoku—Rokudan—Eian or Pinan-Shodan.

High blocks (Jodan-Age-Uke). Edge of the hand at high level (Jodan-Shuto-Barai).
Katas = Taikyoku-Yodan—Taikyoku-Godan—Enpi (elbow).

Middle level blocks (Shudan-Ude-Uke or Uchi-Uke), edge of the hand (Shuto-Uke).
Katas = Taikyoku Sandan—Keri-no-Kata (kicks).

Low blocks (Gedan-Barai) and attacks while in pursuit (Oie-Tsuki).
Katas = Taikyiku-Shodan—Taikyoku Nidan.

This programme, which is not imperative, is based on a young man of about 18-20 years and is susceptible to variation according to age, 12-15 years, or 25-40 years for example, even 50-60 years depending on the frequency of training and the instructor.

The Referees

Before the development and the craze for competition among young people, the Federation has created probationary classes for referees, for perfecting competitive ability and for Katas.

The referees are classified in the following manner:

(1) Student referee.
(2) Probationary referee.
(3) Deputy referee.
(4) National referee.
(5) International referee

The passage from one category to another is made following an examination.
In order to be an association referee it is necessary to hold a Black Belt in Karate.
Up to Brown Belt (1st Kyu), the grades are awarded by the club Professor, of necessity a Black Belt, who acts as a delegate of the National Federation.

Examination for 1st Dan
Pre-Selection Test

The candidate must justify two years of practice and must pass a "Pre-selection Test" when offered by his Professor (he is presented with a card on which his wins are recorded).
The Pre-selection Test consists of a competition in the form of a pool of six, seven or eight contestants (sometimes more) all Black Belt holders (as is the case for 2nd and 3rd Dan). Each candidate must have five contests.
A win (Ippon) scores ten points, a semi-win (Waza-Ari) seven points, a decision five points and a loss scores nil. It is necessary to score 100 points to pass the test satisfactorily (in several competitions, of course) or 44 points in a single competition. This is a test of pre-selection, and many candidates make the error of believing that they "have" or "deserve" the black belt in Karate before passing the test . . . that certain boxers, savate players and other disciplined fighters can also obtain one after a short training intended to teach them respect for the Karate competition rules.
The test indicates minimum efficacy, but not technical worth.

Technical Test

The candidate must give satisfaction in a "Technical Test". It is composed obligatorily of an examination in "pure technique" (Kihon) marked up to 50, and the "forms" (Katas) also marked up to 50. He may also finish up with application of Sanbon-Kumite or Gohon-Kumite at the request of the examiners. It is necessary to obtain at least 30 marks in each section and in a single examination. It is a common error to think that a pass mark of 60/100 is sufficient even though one has under 30 marks in each individual section. The "competition" grade is not confirmed (by the Federation's Committee Director after a proposal by the Federal Commission of Grades) until the delivery of a dossier in which is found the Professor's agreement and a certificate showing that there have been no criminal convictions.
After the age of 30 and in certain special cases (Professors who are handicapped in some way, etc.) a black belt may be awarded without competition.
When a candidate has passed his pre-selection test (efficacy) he may present himself for the Technical Tests in the following month. If he fails he cannot re-enter for two months, and if he fails again, he can re-enter every four months.
It would no doubt be very useful for candidates and future examiners to know the eliminating faults which can seriously affect a candidate's average. This advice comes from my own personal experience as the most senior member of the Grades Commission and from my studies in Japan. The following qualities and advice are valid for all styles and Schools.

Execution:

In addition to the advice given above concerning presentation, if during the execution of a Kata or Kihon you give the sign for retirement (on realising an error, for example), this is given no marks. Even if you have mistaken the order or a movement, continue to do your best until the end. Then, making your apologies politely ask the examiners for permission to execute the correct Kata or the movement demanded (in general, the examiner knows what confusion can be caused by the Japanese names and will accede to the request if it is correctly formulated, without you rubbing your head, putting your tongue out or assuming a false air of despair).

The aim of Karate being the attainment of self-control in the course of combats more impressive than those of a promotion contest, you have no excuse to find, even that of examination nerves. Keep a frank, clear and direct look.

Look:

It must remain alive, attentive at Yoi and concentrated during the execution (faults: closing the eyes when blocking an attack, looking towards the ground or otherwise than at the real or imaginary opponent).

Breathing:

Except in certain Katas, this should not be visible during execution or combat, loud or silent Kiais at impact or moments of maximum concentration. Faults: to make a visible respiration during a Kata, in the course of executing a movement, the mouth open at certain times. Avoid grimaces.

Hips:

1. They must not be raised during a block or an attack. 2. They should practically always be horizontal (faults: the advanced hip higher or lower than the rear hip in Ko-Kutsu, Zen-Kutsu, etc.).

Abdomen:

A strong lower abdomen is a quality of the Black Belt. That is to say, the abdomen (around the navel) must be strong, tensed, in line with the chest, stomach solid. Your marks will immediately drop if you relax this region with the pelvis uncontrolled (it must be upright, back level, the buttocks pulled in and strong).

Shoulders:

The same as above. If your shoulders are raised, without strength in the arms, your power will leave your abdomen and stomach . . . and your marks will drop.

Legs:

They must be strong. This seems self-evident, but many candidates fail, losing their balance in the course of the Katas, having the advanced knee unsteady and without strength, the rear leg weak (whether it is extended or slightly bent, it must be strong). You must be firm during blocks and your attacks, whether you are alone or with an opponent (or examiner).

Feet:

The necessity to be steady on your legs brings with it regard for the position of the feet; turned slightly inwards in Zen-Kutsu, for example, or the rear foot slightly forwards (and not towards the rear) in Ko-Kutsu or Zen-Kutsu, the two feet turned inwards in Sanchin-Dachi, in Kiba-Dachi. These rules are equally valid for Wado-Ryu, Shito-Ryu, Goju-Ryu or Shotokan.

Purity:
All these Karate Schools seek after a purity of attack such as when one releases the string of a bow. It is obvious if you make a warning movement of the advanced foot (if you turn it before advancing or executing an action, flex and then extend the rear leg before advancing it, change your breathing, contract your face, blink your eyes, lower your fist BEFORE attacking, you will be telegraphing to your opponents what you intend to do. While you make these warning movements in Kihon or in the Katas executed "one for one" you cannot pretend to be entering into Karate.

Therefore, to obtain good marks.

Concentration of force:
Equally common to all the schools for black-belt, the concentration of force at the end of a block, attack or counter-attack must be TOTAL (fist perfectly clenched and correct, the power coming from the rear foot in the majority of cases) with a brief period of time for penetration (Kime).

Dead time:
While you are seeking purity and speed, it is evident that periods of hesitation will lower your marks considerably. For instance, if you leave your hand at your ear or hip too long in certain blocks or attacks. The first object is to parry or to strike the opponent, not to make motions which may perhaps be part of the "forms", but are inapplicable. But, when you have passed to black belt, that is the time to make applicable motions. At any rate, after you have begun to attain the beginnings of speed you will eliminate most of the periods of dead time. There must be no more hesitation between the block and the counter-attack.

Sincerity:
You should attack and block with conviction. To perform the Katas at combat speed or "one for one" without mistaking the order shows that you have been training regularly, but the conviction, the sincerity, this shows the level of attainment, that is to say, the interior feeling in relation to external appearances.

The motions of blocking, attacking and of the combinations must respect the norms of each school, this is obvious, and not to pass the left arm over the right arm for Jodan-Age-Uke on the left, for example, is a serious fault for it then becomes Uraken. But the motions must be complete. In combat, we all shorten our blows through emotion or excitement, but obviously the more complete (not curtailed) they are, the more powerful and effective they will be. In Kata as in Kihon, it is necessary to strive for perfection, then when you are in an examination, try to perform as completely and as perfectly as possible.

The upper body:
Again we have a quality common to all Karate styles, the upper part of the body must be held perfectly erect, upright, for you must be able to pivot freely and parry attacks in the best way (if your upper body is bent forwards, the attacks with the feet that you may receive will strike your chest at right angles instead of sliding off as is the case when the attack is imperfect). According to the style, the upper body is found more or less sideways on to the attack or into the attack. Nevertheless, it is the rule that it should be face on—or almost so—in attack, and turned slightly sideways in defence.

As you see, the examiner—this is the moment to say it—does not quibble over petty details, but basing himself on general principles he looks for the level of the candidate's "quality". He may base his judgement on a general feeling, only keeping in mind the candidate's qualities (his progress), or by regarding the faults in relation to an overall efficacy. This is what you should do when looking at a senior or an expert. Seek the qualities in preference to the faults.

Pool Tables

It is a good thing to familiarize yourself with the examination techniques, re-create them in the Dojo and develop a fighting spirit by means of pool competitions, which are very interesting besides.

But the complexity of the pools makes improvisation impossible. I think, therefore, that many will be satisfied to find below the order of pool contests for six, seven and eight contestants. This order permits each contestant a rest period of from one to three bouts between each contest, and assures that each has five contests.

To read the following table, it must be understood that: In a pool of six, contestant number one meets number two, then number three meets number four, and so on.

Pool of Six	Pool of Seven (1)	Pool of Nine
1—2	2—6	1—2
3—4	3—5	3—5
2—6	4—7	6—8
1—5	1—2	1—4
4—6	3—6	2—7
2—3	4—5	3—6
1—6	2—7	1—5
4—5	1—3	2—4
1—3	4—6	7—8
2—5	5—7	1—3
3—6	2—3	2—5
1—4	1—4	4—6
3—5	5—6	3—7
2—4	3—7	5—8
5 6	2—4	1—6
	1—5	4—7
	6—7	3—8
		2—6
		5—7
		4—8

(1) Draw lots for No. 1 who has only four contests but who can be made to fight twice.

4. The Katas (Forms)

For a spectator, a Karate Kata is a strange affair. The Karateka attacks the air with a terrible expression in his eyes, his muscles knotted, uttering alarming cries from time to time. His motions often appear to be very beautiful and realistic, even without understanding the spectator is respectful and admiring, but sometimes he has to hold back an almost irresistible desire to laugh when seeing the queer-looking gestures, "catching flies", hearing the little animal noises.

The difference comes from the practitioner's level, which should express something in his motions, as a musician should express something in his interpretation at the risk of putting his audience to sleep.

Each Kata always begins with a defence, expressing in this way the non-violence of Karate. It contains a certain number of typical defences and attacks. Of course, there are other methods of evading, diverting or attacking in the Karate repertoire, but those of the Katas are the most educational.

In a Kata, one should never feel oneself to be weak, without tension of the spirit. Under no circumstances should one, by one's own fault, permit a position of deliberate weakness, FOR THE OPPONENT WILL NOT EXCUSE IT! If one appreciates this, the Kata becomes true, even if one still makes "apparent faults".

Even if one has not yet acquired the true feeling of Kata—this demands several years—so that the order comes naturally, it is necessary to SEARCH for the idea of the Kata and "see" the phantom opponents, sense their advance, their deadly attacks BEFORE moving. And when blocking, do not just try to stop the blow, but also unbalance and weaken (injure) the opponents. To learn the order and seek to apply the correct postures, on the surface, without feeling inside, is an error. Because you learn the postures in Kihon so as to be able to execute them in the Katas more spontaneously and with feeling. In the same way as you learn the musical notes in order eventually to give them life through the written staves. The Katas must always be executed with desperation, a sense of drama, without attaching too much importance to the correction of petty details. You have the rest of your life for that. If you seek after the appearance before the feeling, there are few chances that you will one day be able to introduce a genuine sensation of combat. The eyes must at no time leave the imaginary opponent to look at the ground or the place which is being attacked. At no time must one become weaker, on the contrary it is necessary to feel stronger and stronger yet, violent, as the Kata unfolds to its end, with one or two peaks which are in general accompanied by the Kiai.

At the beginning (Yoi) and at the last movement (where one rests for one second) it is necessary to feel that one is ready to block in all directions.

Sensing the Opponent

While blocking or attacking in Kata, it is necessary to "feel" the opponent clearly each time, and simultaneously to feel the presence of other adversaries, this is one of the reasons why the upper body must be kept quite upright, balanced. Blocks, attacks and evolutions (above all when one turns or pivots) must be performed as a single, unified action, all of a sudden, very fast (even if one errs a little, this is normal when trying to do better). The unity of action takes precedence over the action's speed: a single pure and relatively slow action is faster than a rapid action preceded by a warning movement, not only in actual time (by chronometer) but also in terms of the opponent (if he can be anticipated or surprised) . . . It is necessary also to find the rhythm of combat, avoiding the same monotonous cadence and seeking a respiration which must give nothing away.

One sees by these examples how useful Kata is for "moulding" the body and spirit, how thrilling it becomes when one has understood its aims. In fact, the possibilities for progress are unlimited.

If one is quite alone and has the bases of Karate, one can continue to progress to a high level. If one has none of these bases and has studied by means of books, but has practised a great many Katas with sincerity and every day (at least 20 daily) at combat speed, one must eventually finish by re-joining the true Karate. In executing the Katas, separating the motions "one by one", one has a tendency to accentuate the little warning movements and faults, and establish them in the body.

There are not two Karates, that of the Katas-Kihon and that of free combat. In the beginning, it seems impossible to fight with the same style because the body becomes excited and the movements become incomplete, disordered with fear, anger and excitement. But it is precisely in order to fight deep, concentrated, strong, stable and fast that one trains in Kata. The two must finish by becoming alike in a few years (three to ten years). A true Kata should be a real combat. With all the mental and physical energy.

Moulding the Body

The Katas are equally aimed at "moulding" the body. Also, one generally recovers the ability to perform on the right that which one performs on the left, for harmonious development.

One can execute the Katas a certain number of times "in purity", a certain number of times in "total contraction", some muscles opposing active muscles, finishing by 10 to 20 extensions at combat speed with 30 seconds to one minute of rest (breathing for complete oxygenization).

In the beginning you will be very tired, you may even want to be sick or to faint. You must force yourself and find the means of holding on (notably by muscular co-ordination and breathing). Afterwards, it will be better. Then you will again be very fatigued because having become "wound-up" anew, you will really employ all your energy . . . but if you persevere, you will break through a certain ceiling and enter an exciting stage.

You will find in the pages that follow the principal basic Katas. We can do no better in this small manual than to give you the order. This will be an aid to the memory by means of pictures. If you wish to penetrate further, turn to my book "Manual of Karate for Black Belt" (to obtain the black belt) which describes them in detail and speaks of advanced, alleged secrets of Karate, with much advice for training.

Perhaps you are frightened by the number of Katas. In fact, the order is a small matter. One can learn in a few days. In the course of our Summer and Winter classes, I see many beginners learn 10 to 15 Katas easily. All the work starts afterwards.

It is necessary to learn a large number of Katas, for their execution trains you in the same movements: these are the basic movements contained in all the Katas. In a parallel way, it is necessary for you to concentrate on a single Kata, your favourite, and it is this that you execute a great many times at combat speed in order to feel its spirit. Then the other Katas will come to you one day and your progress will be rapid. It is not a good thing to have a false modesty and to say "I prefer to execute one Kata, and do that one well" and to know but a few. It is, on the contrary, necessary to "understand" the greatest number possible (good for the memory) and to repeat them often (if not, one forgets them, this is a good way of compelling yourself to train for one sees immediately that one has lost something, at least the order), and to break through the one that pleases you the most to get the "feeling".

In the photographs that follow you have a correct execution of the Katas. If you are of an advanced level, you will certainly notice some very small faults, for everybody and the black belts also still have further to progress. But you will note many qualities among my friends Nanbu, Mochizuki, and my students Bahu, Baroux, Caujolle, Lavorato, Ribert and Trann whom I thank here, for an honest Karateka does not particularly like to be photographed. To be photographed sometimes shows in effect an excessive satisfaction . . . but not to let oneself be photographed is without doubt also an indication of a lack of modesty. Many thanks for their courtesy, already well known in the Dojo.

Kata, which means "form" is, as its name implies, a series of pre-arranged attacks and defences in a given order, always the same. It is a sort of rhythmic or war dance. In fact, it is more than this, it is an educational DRAMA, a DESPERATE struggle against several opponents (8 or 10) who are trying to kill you.

A wonderful, pure Kata which can be executed alone or with a partner. It is the most profound of the Katas (Pages 86-88).

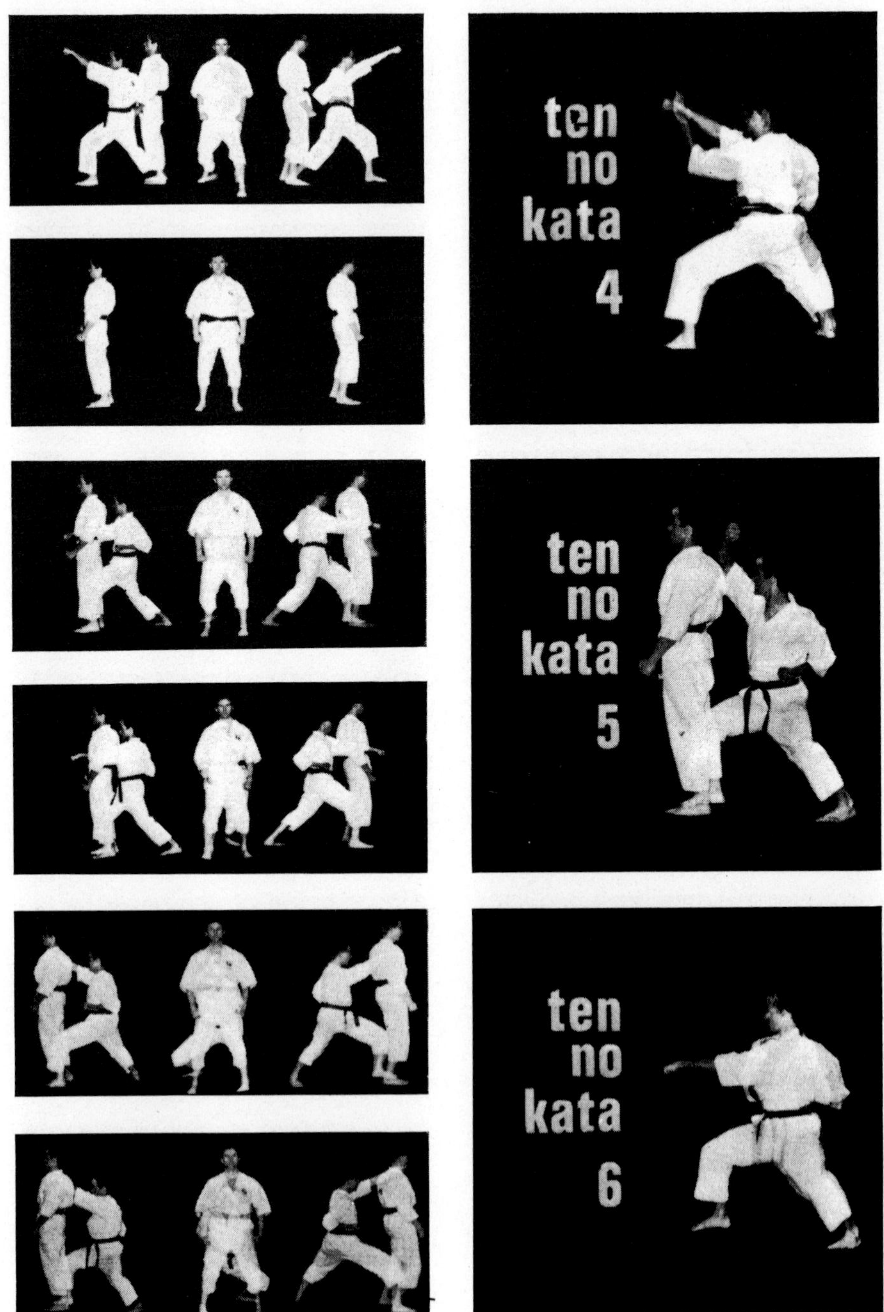

ten
no
kata
4
ten
no
kata
5
ten
no
kata
6

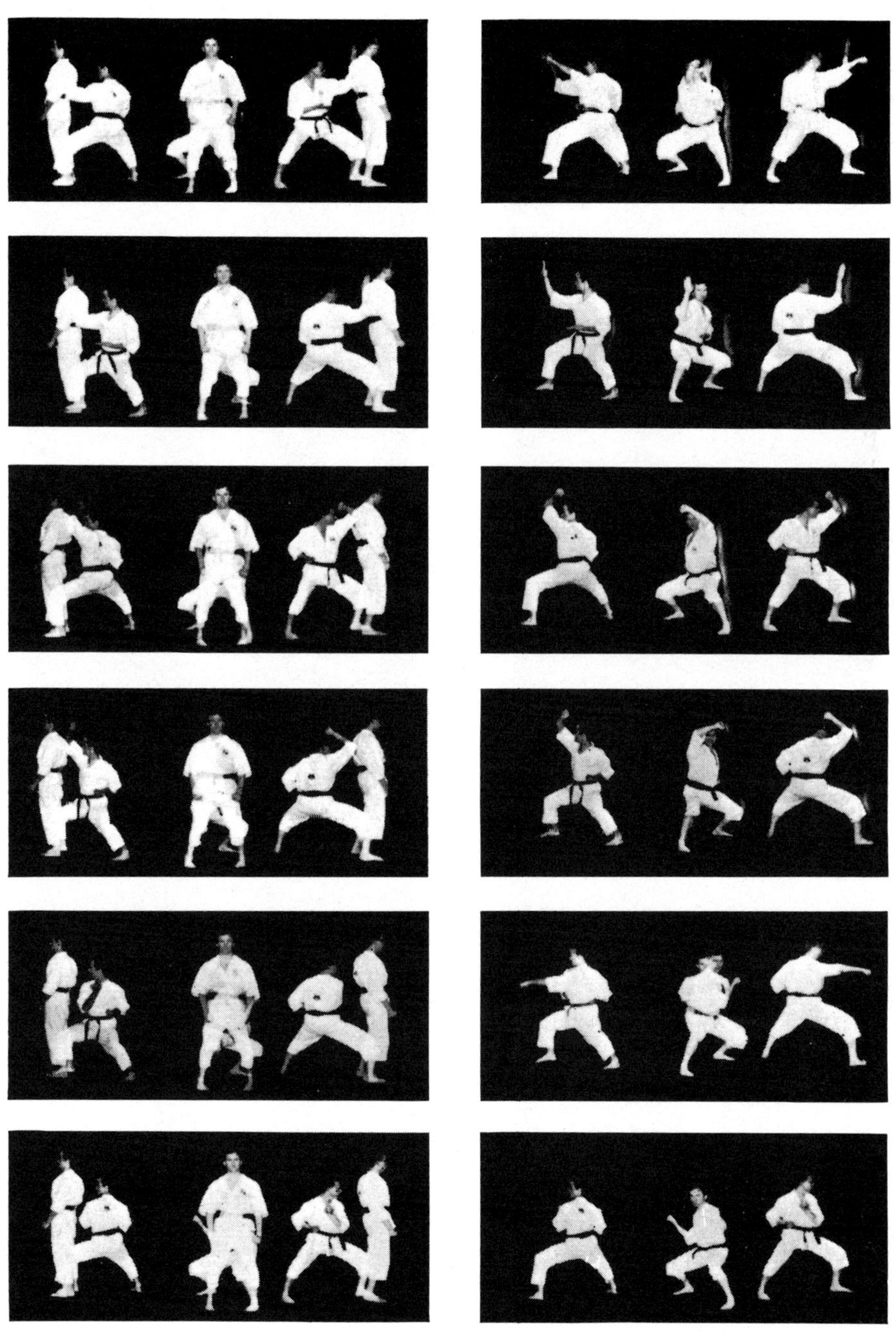

taikyoku shodan

This Kata forms part of a series of six Katas aimed at general development. It is very important for the execution of the perfect Eian Katas (and the most ancient Katas). It develops on an H-shaped course and is composed solely of low blocks (Gedan-Barai) and middle level attacks. The development of Taikyoku on the ground is clearly seen on pages 92, 93 and 94.

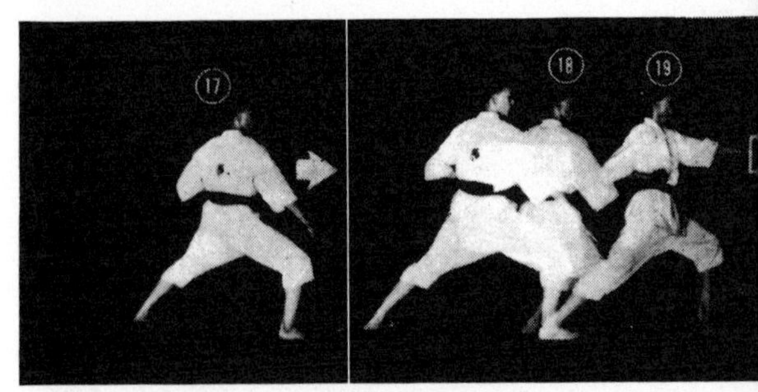

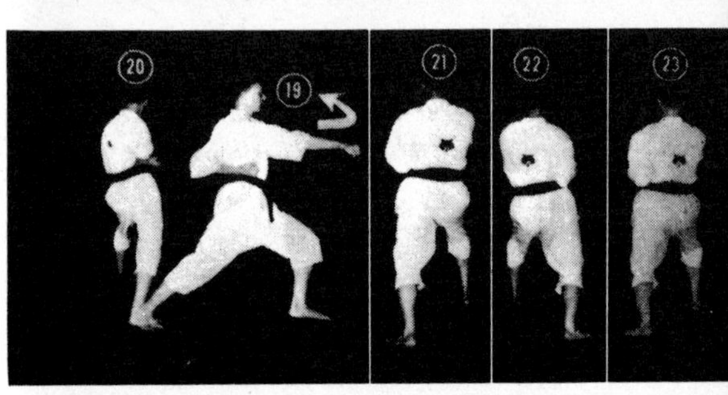

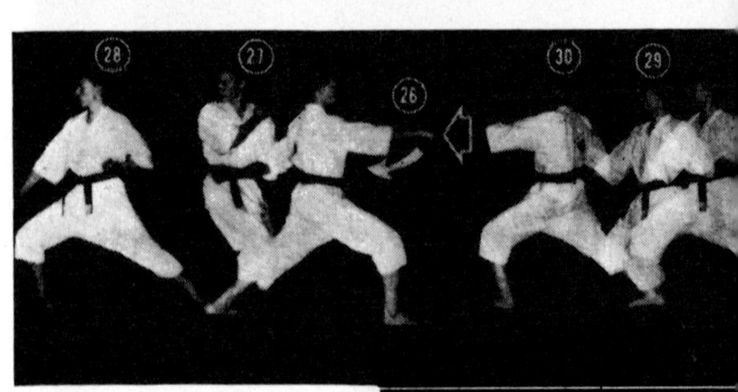

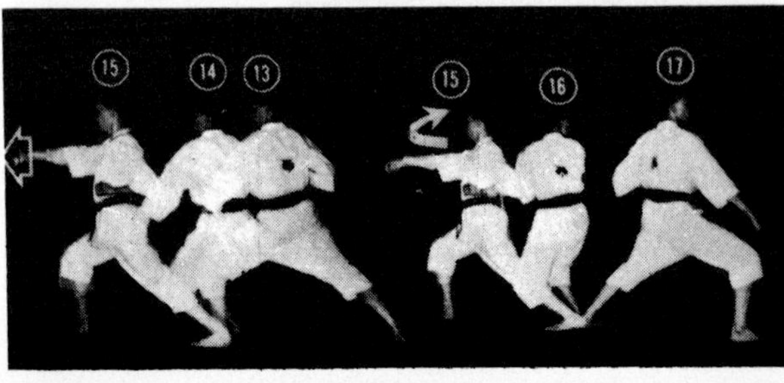

This is just the same as the first Taikyoku, save for the fact that the three central attacks are higher when moving out from the starting point (10, 11 and 12 with Kiai) and when returning (21, 22 and 23 with Kiai) instead of being middle level as in the preceding Kata. The three central attacks are a preparation for Sanbon-Kumite and must be executed in the same spirit.

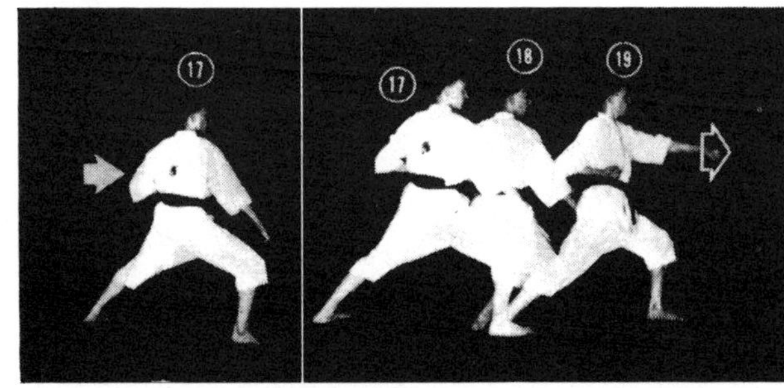

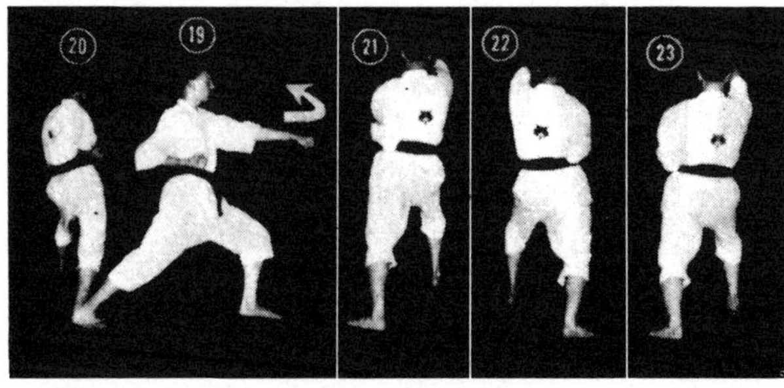

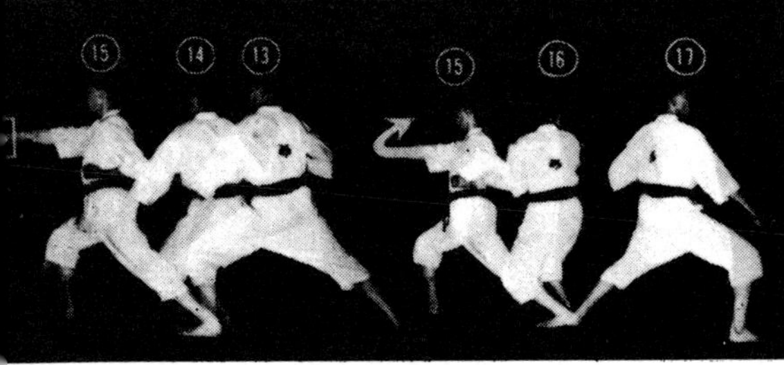

Here, the difference from the two first Taikyoku is that the third is performed in Kokutsu for the blocks, except for the two preparatory Gedan-Barai to three attacks in succession (Sanbon-Kumite) on the axis of the H. It is very difficult to perform a real Kokutsu which is generally turned into a half Zenkutsu. So watch out. As for the other Taikyoku, the attacks are performed in Oie-Tsuki-Zen-Kutsu.

taikyoku yodan

Everything is high level: blocks and attacks. The important difference from the first three is that the blocks (Jodan-Age-Uke) are performed very rapidly in half Zen-Kutsu, in "combat" style. In place of the three middle or high level attacks, one executes three blows with the elbow while moving out from the starting point (10, 11 and 12 with Kiai) and three at high level (15, 16 and 17 with Kiai) on the return. An excellent preparation for Eian-Shodan.

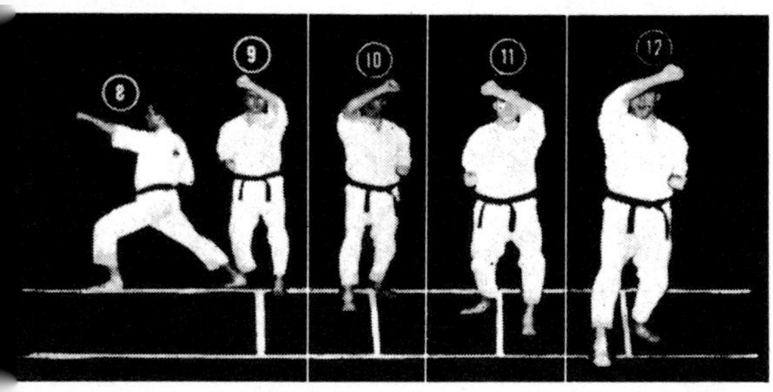

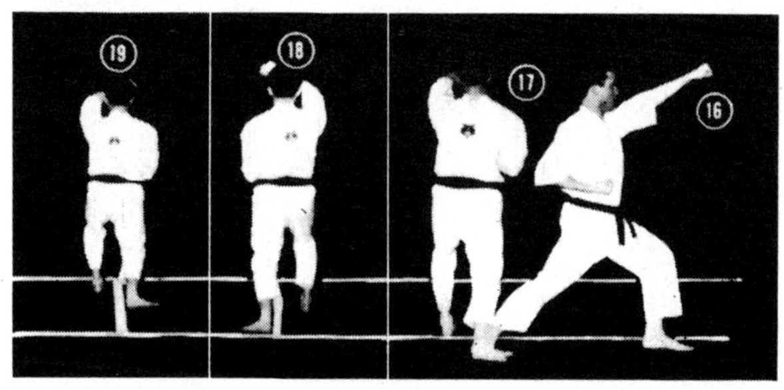

Everything is middle level. Block in half Zen-Kutsu as in the fourth Taikyoku (but you can of course also do it in a deep Zenkutsu) followed by a long, penetrating Oie-Tsuki. Three Tsuki at middle level when moving out from the starting point as in Taikyoku Shodan (and not blocks as in the fourth) with a Kiai on the third. The same on the return.

The interesting features are the speed of the blocks, performed almost on the spot, followed by very long, powerful attacks. The three last Taikyoku are also performed very slowly, contracted, with deep respiration.

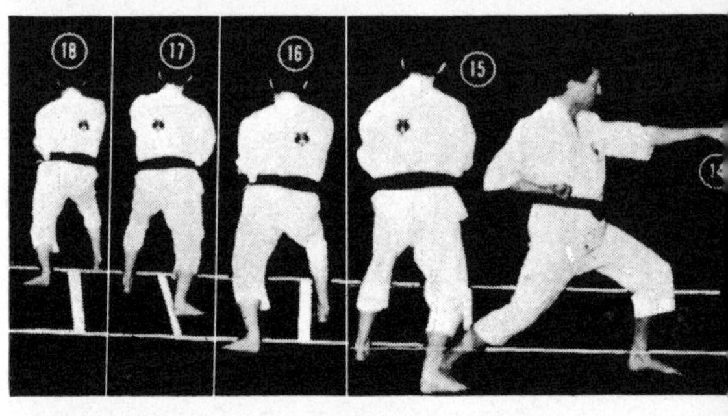

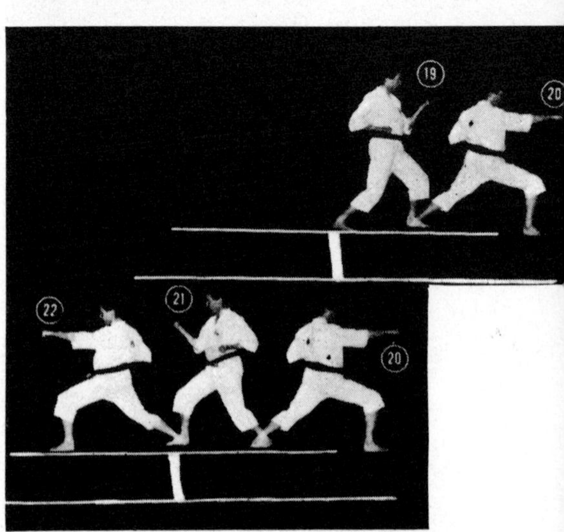

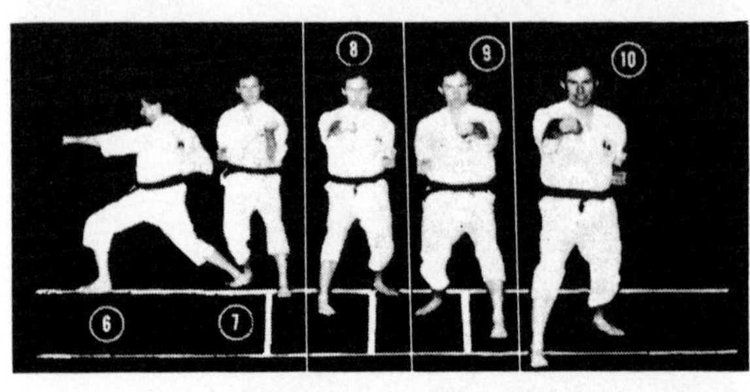

Everything is at very low level. The first Gedan-Barai signifies an attack with the side of the fist (Tetsui) at the lower abdomen. The second, another attack or one kick followed by an attack on the other side. It is, with the first, the most interesting of the Taikyoku.

All the Taikyoku can be performed with bare hands or armed with a baton held two-handed (about 4ft. 6in.), a knife or a Sai (a sort of trident originating in Okinawa).

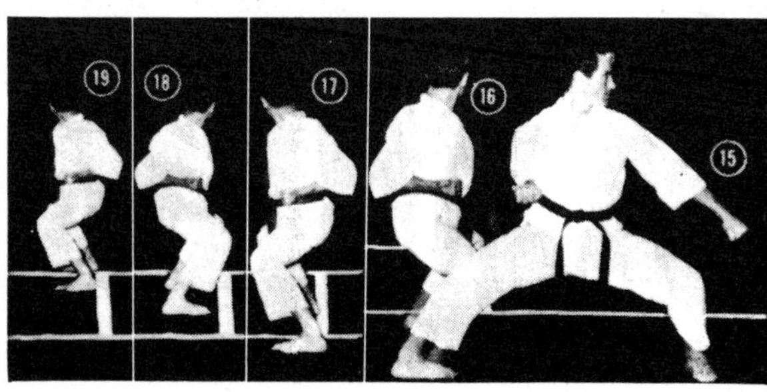

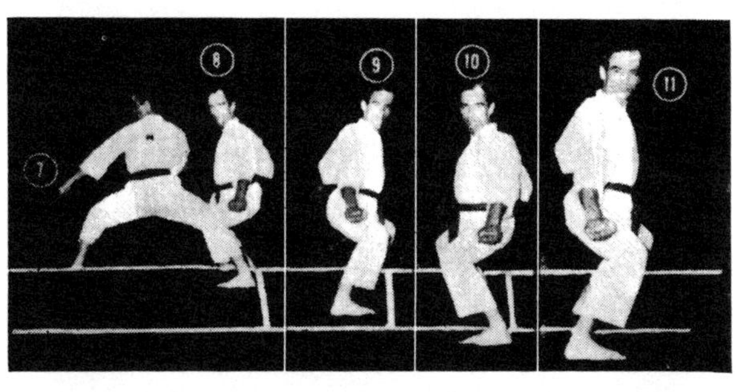

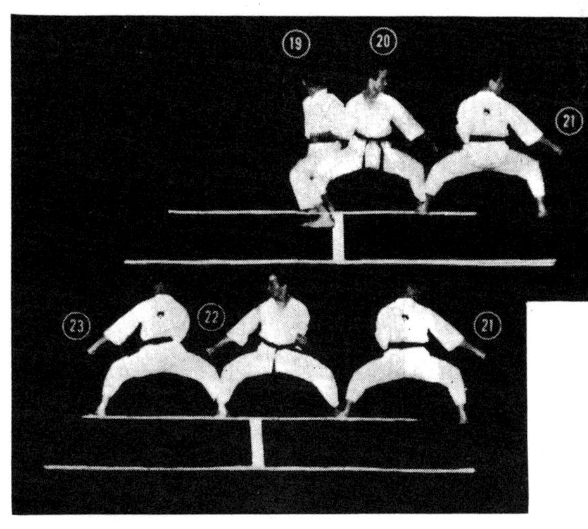

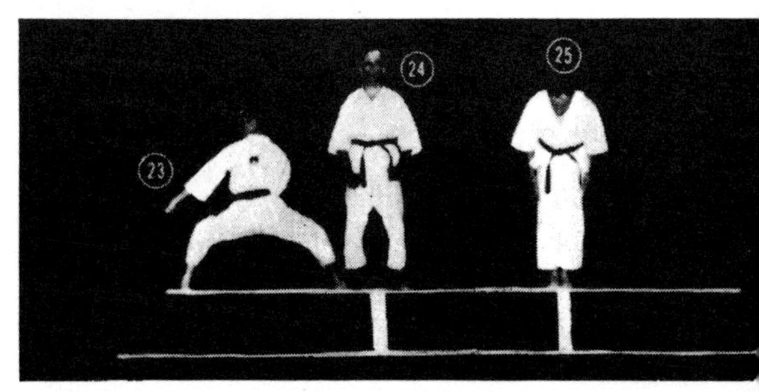

eian shodan

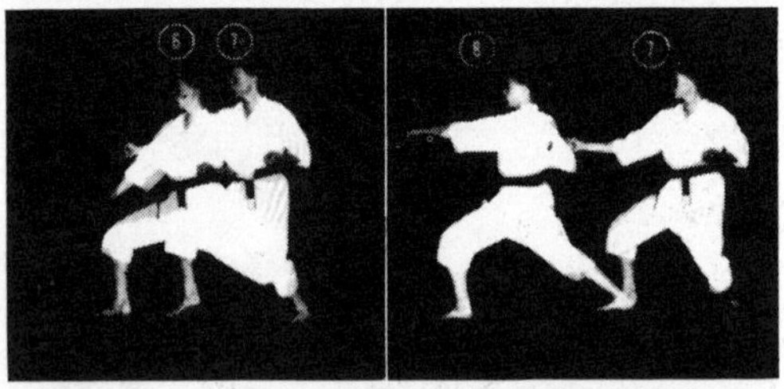

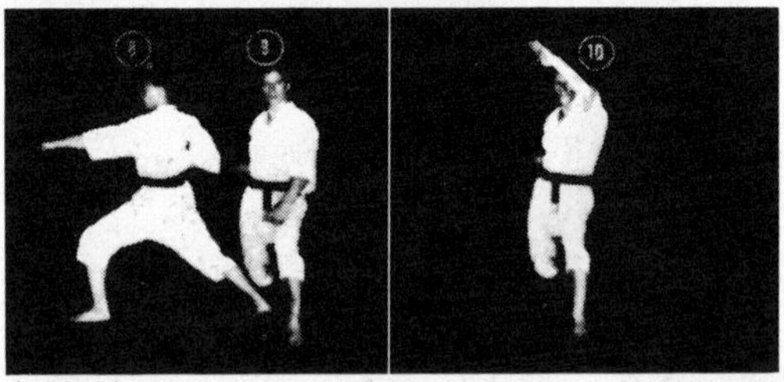

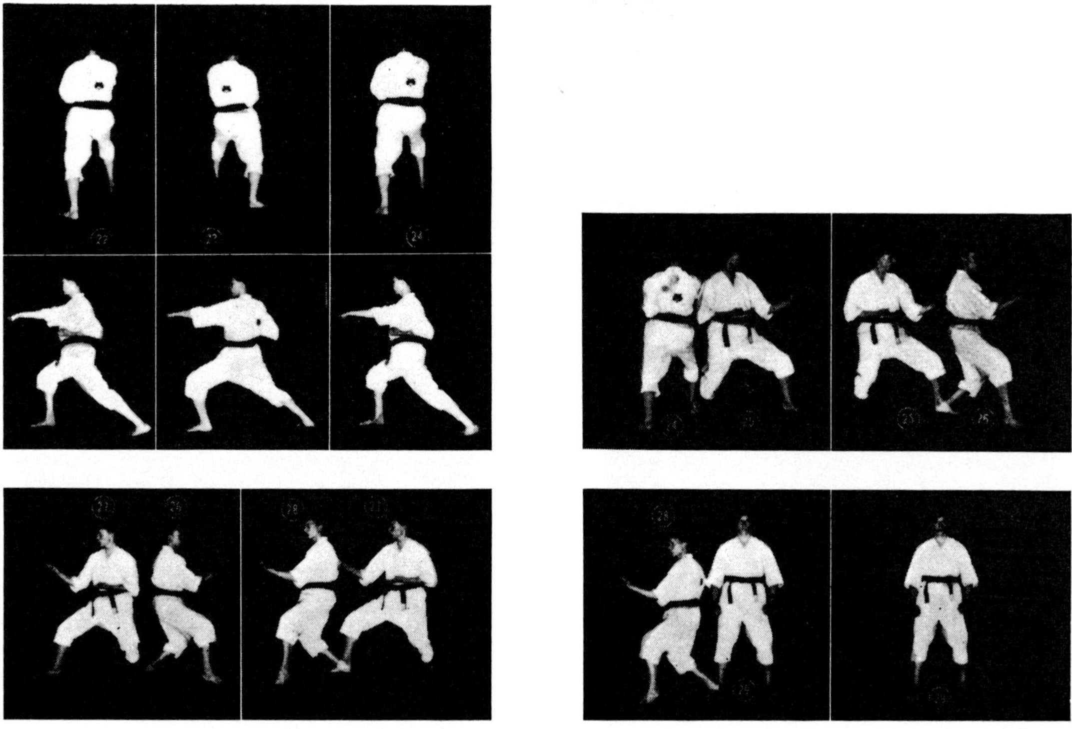

The five Eian are essential for 1st Dan in France and in most of the countries of Europe (or the Pinan according to the Schools). You must study them very seriously. But if you have had considerable practice with the six Taikyoku, this will be very simple.

It differs from Taikyoku 1 and 4 only in that the Shuto (blocks with the edge of the hand) in the last four movements (25-26-27-28) are executed one for one (four adversaries) and not with the idea of a "one-two" (block-attack). And the three attacks while moving out from the starting point as well as the three on the return on the H have a different rhythm: this is not so much a training in Sanbon-Kumite as in Taikyoku, but an interpretation of real combat. In general, one thinks of blocking, then attacking with the elbow, and the other defends himself. After a short pause—surprise or concentration—one attacks rapidly twice in succession with the elbow when moving out and with the fist on the return.

But you can interpret the rhythm in a different way, if only to clarify what you wish to convey (as in the case of a personal interpretation of a melody or a dance).

During the period of time between 5 and 6, make a large circle with the arm while pivoting slightly from the hips (more than in Pinan-Nidan 8-9-10), but without letting the hips rise. All the Katas should also develop without any lift of the hips, or almost none.

eian nidan

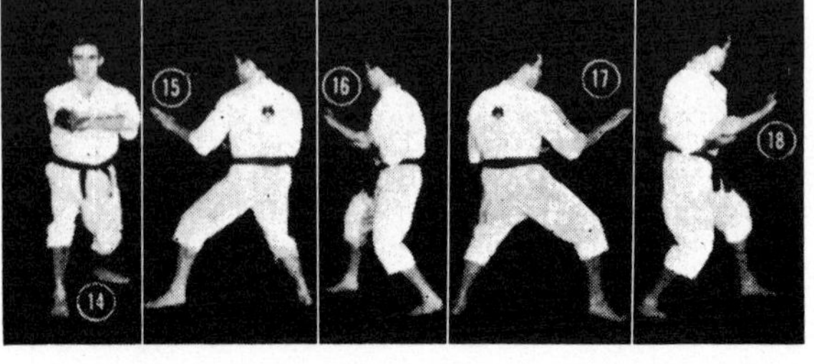

The second Nidan is more complicated. It is impossible
describe otherwise than by long, illustrated explanations (s
the following Manuals).
Nevertheless, if an Instructor has already taught you th
Kata, you will easily recall the order with the aid of t
accompanying illustrations.
In former times, this Eian Nidan was classified as the First.
was the Master Funakoshi who changed the order becau
he considered that No. 1 was easier and more instructiv
He then simplified the Eian Shodan in creating the Taikyo

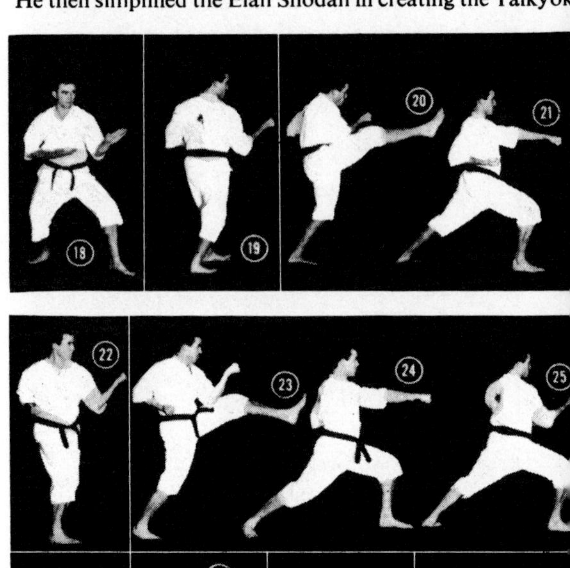

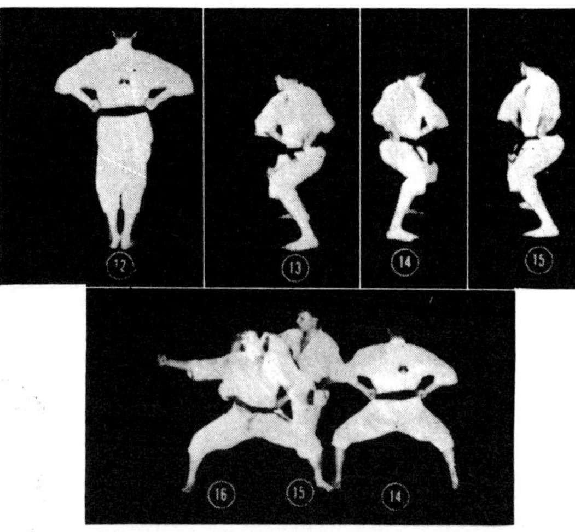

eian sandan

With the first Eian, the third is the easiest, at least to remember, for the more a Kata is devoid of frills the easier it is to see the faults.

The Taikyoku (sixth) will certainly have given you a good, strong Kiba-Dachi, so that this Kata will not present any important difficulties.

The first three blocks are Ude-Uke on the left, then Ude Uke on the right at the same time as Gedan-Barai (two, then three-four).

Here also, it is impossible to unravel the difficulties of this attractive Kata in a few lines.

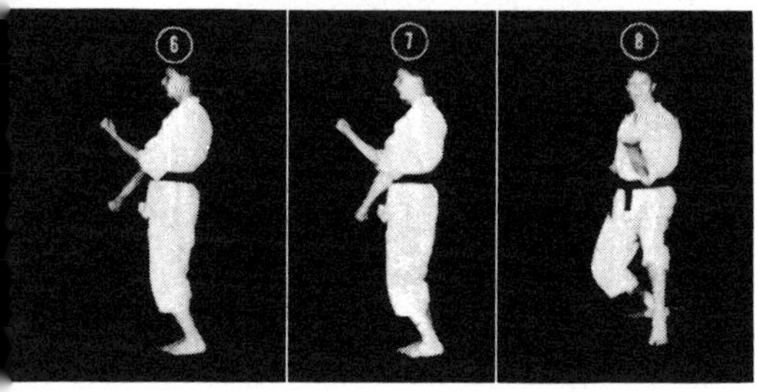

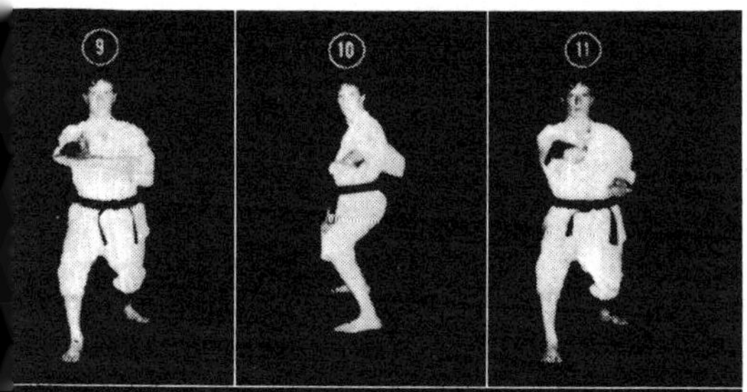

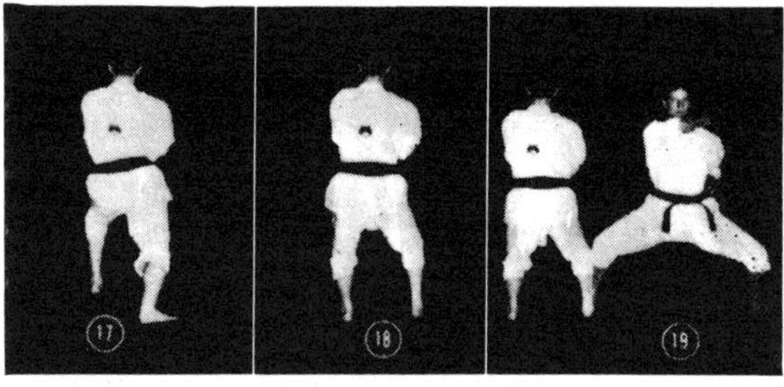

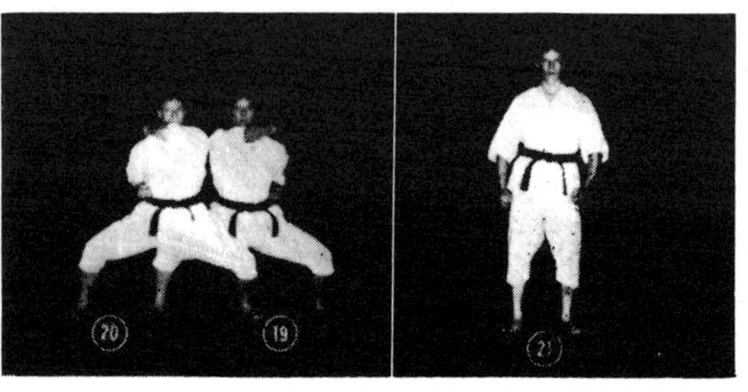

The 4th Eian is, with the 5th, one of the most beautiful, even though some "fall in love" with the 4th. If it seems ridiculous to you to fall in love with a Kata which you probably find tedious, you are just beginning, but persevere and you will understand. The kicks to the side are not performed as one habitually does in combat (penetrating Kekomi) but are rising kicks to the side (Keage) exactly as in Jodan-Age-Uke.

This Kata is full of difficulties which must be studied in detail.

eian   yodan

Eian Godan

A very beautiful Kata from the antique Passai and Kanku.

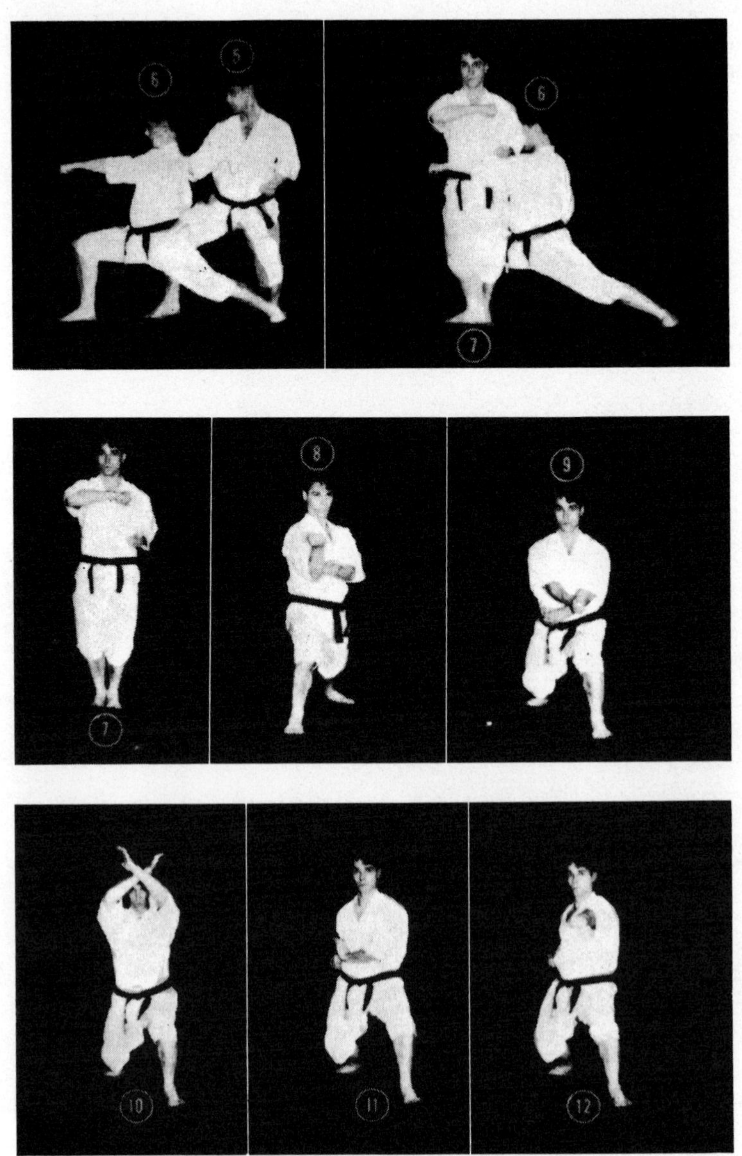

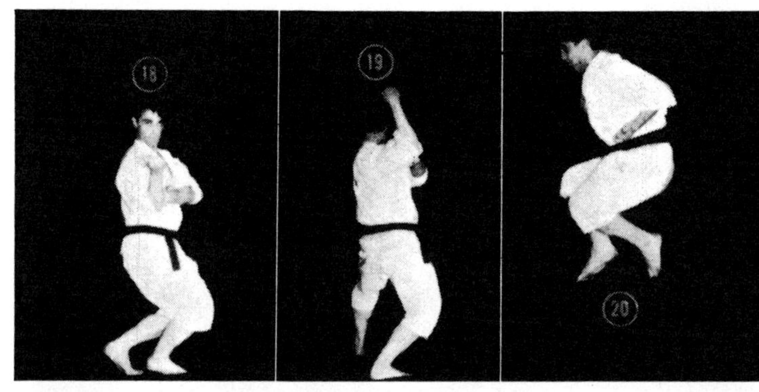

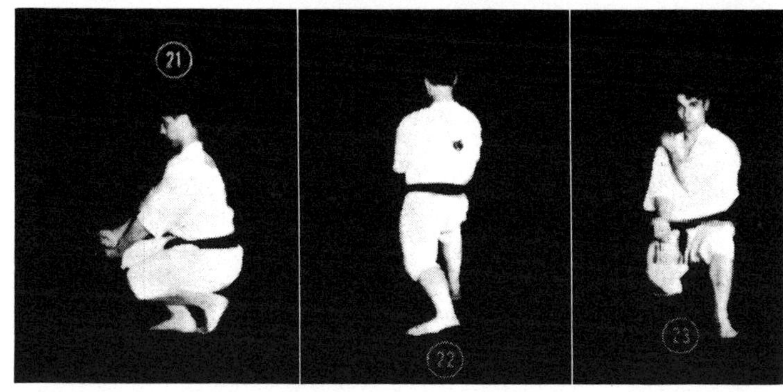

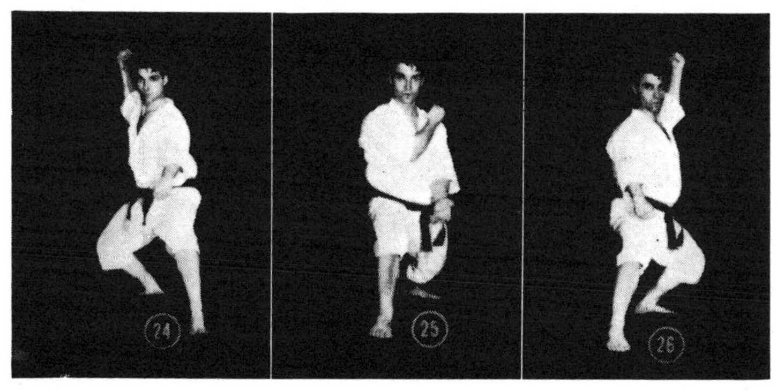

pinan shodan

Similar to Eian-Nidan, in general the blocks are higher. The differences are too involved to explain here. Refer to the following Manual.

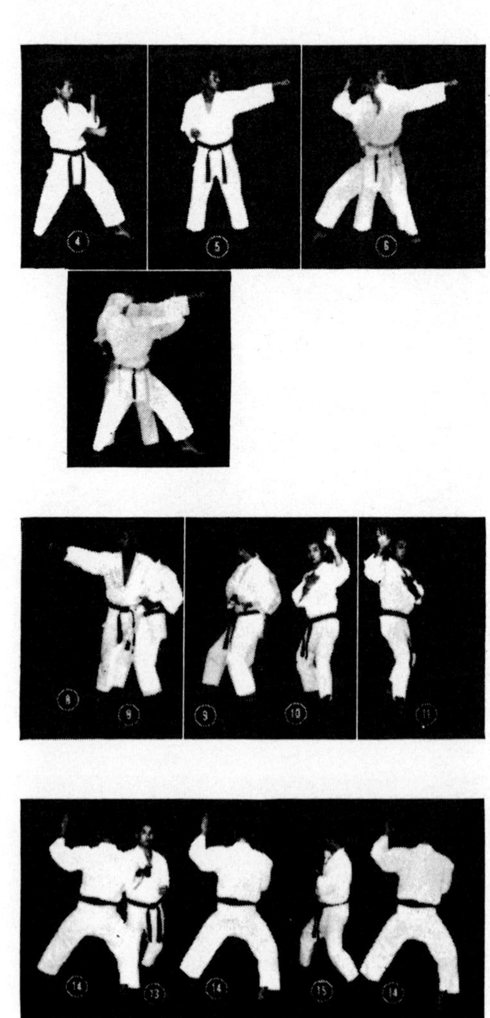

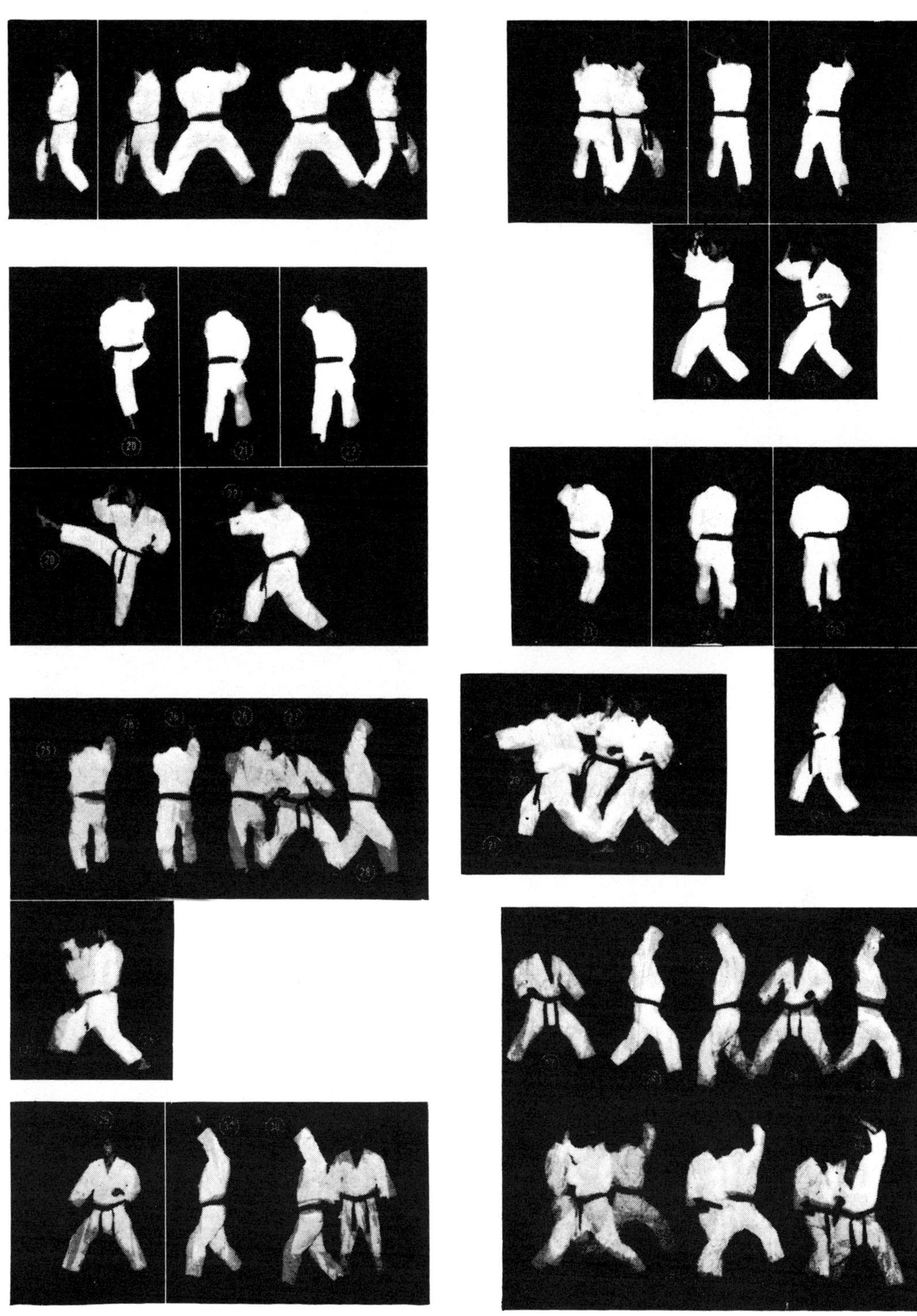

Similar to Eian-Shodan with several differences of interpretation.

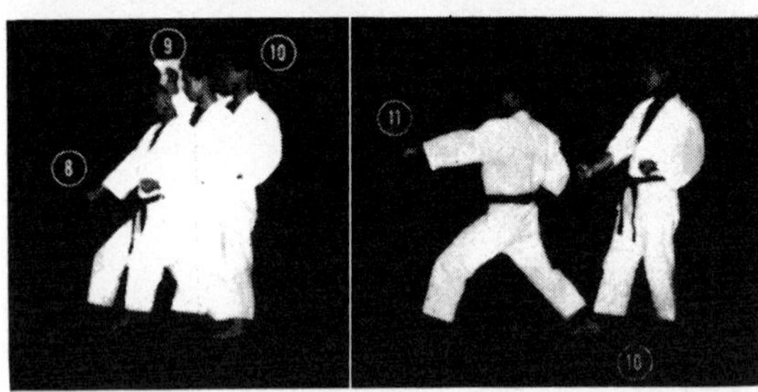

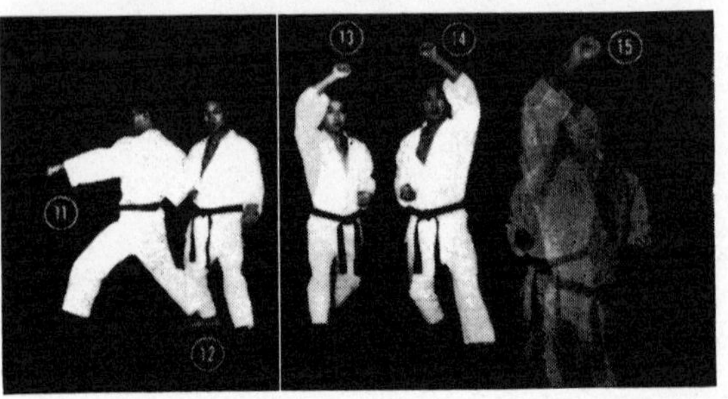

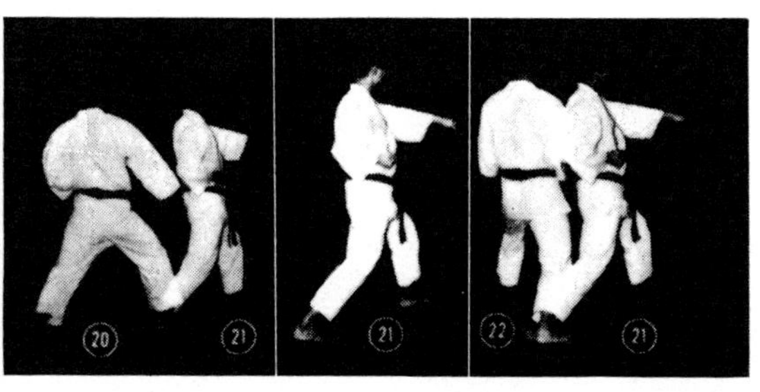

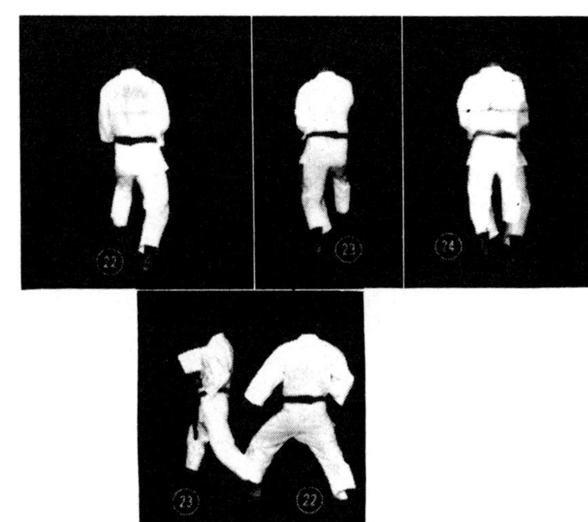

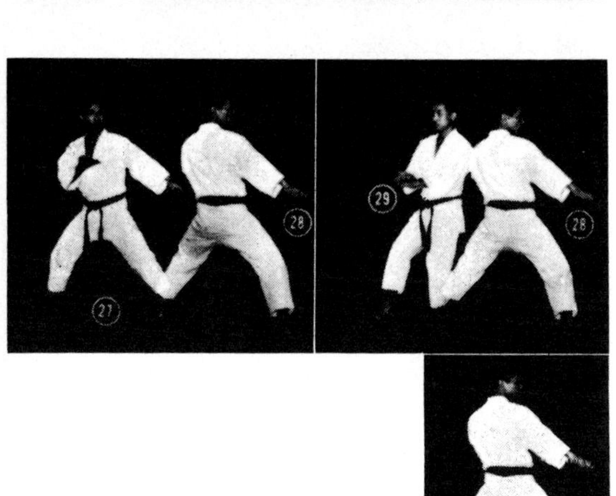

pinan   sandan

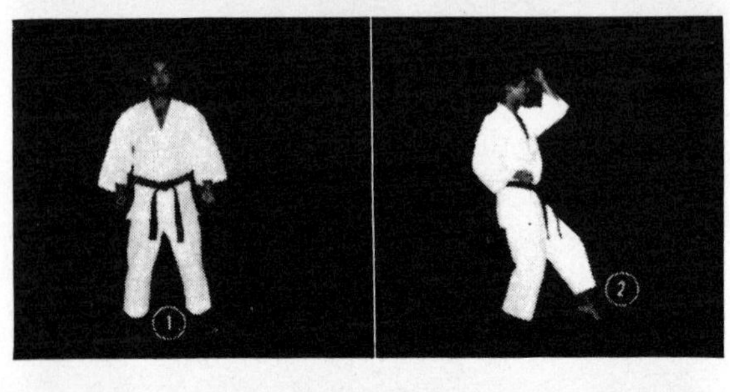

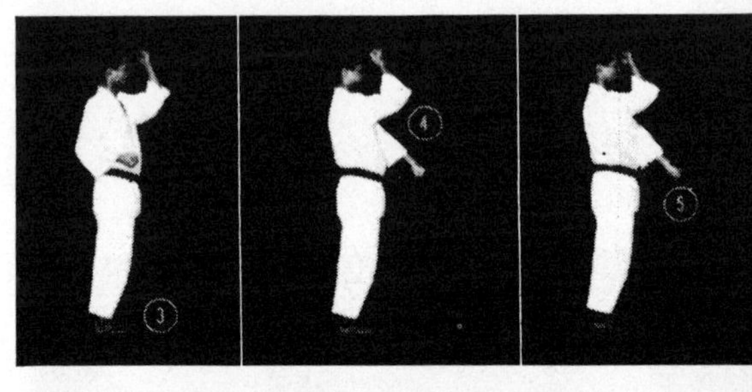

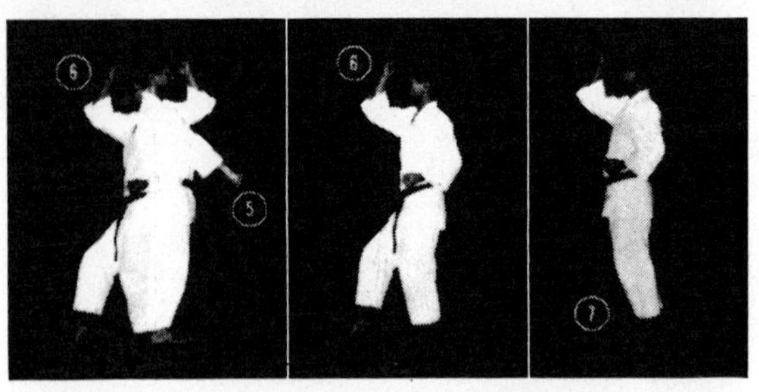

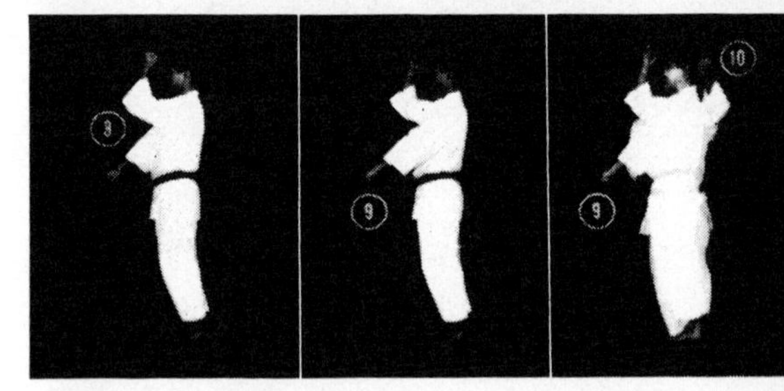

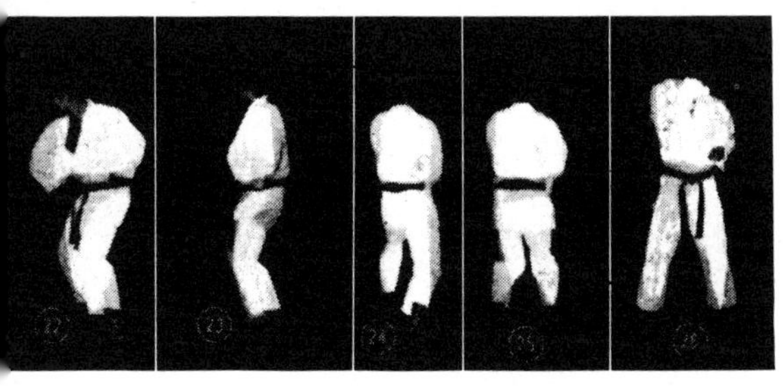

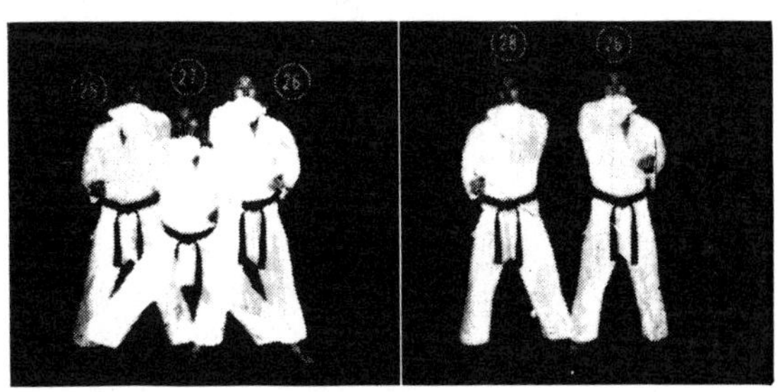

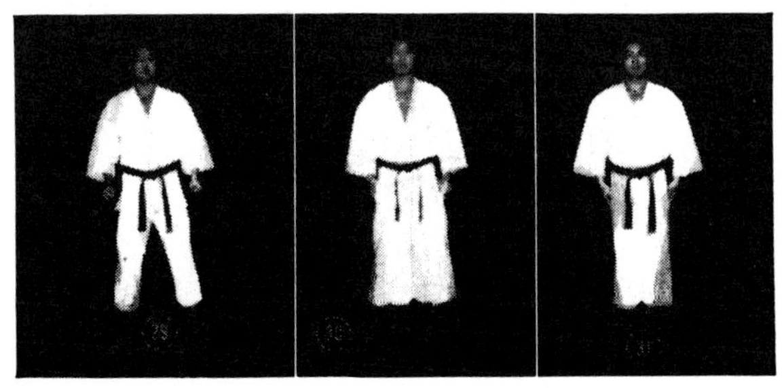

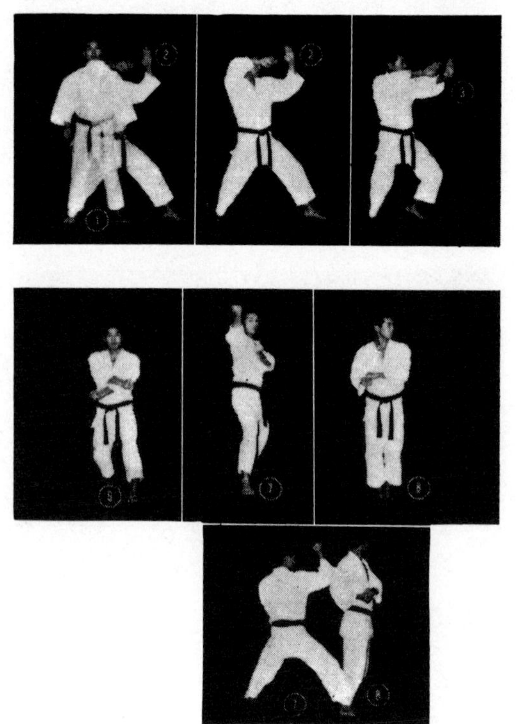

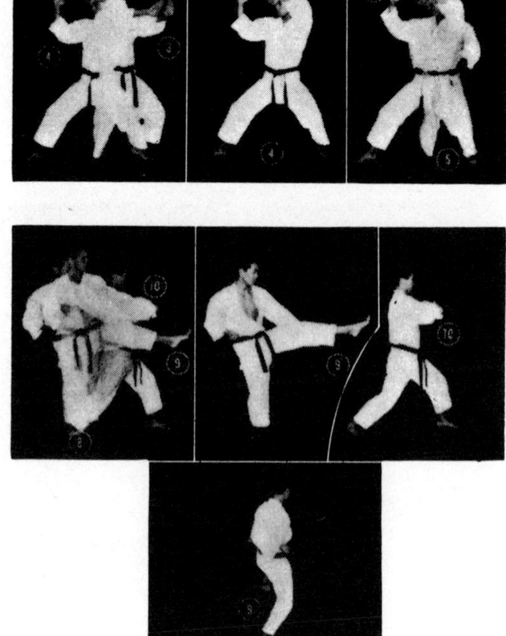

110

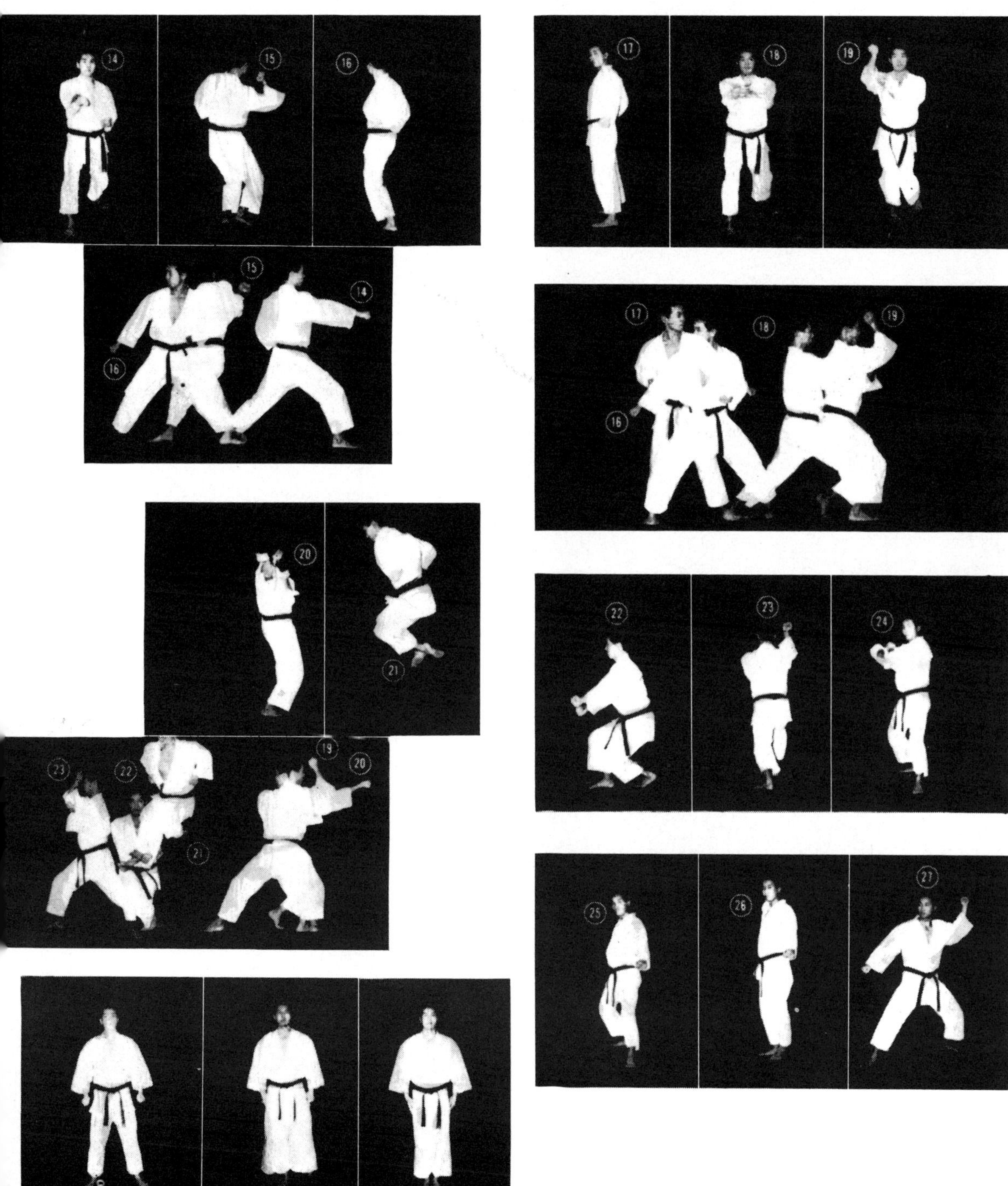

There are six Shihozuki, all extremely interesting, especially the last two where one blocks with the same hand at two different levels before countering with the foot.

The Shihozuki express, as in the Ten-no-Kata (page 79), the blocks while withdrawing from the attack (this is often essential when the attack is pure) instead of advancing to the attack as in the three first Taikyoku, or blocking from the spot as in the 4th and 5th Taikyoku. In practising these Katas one therefore exercises oneself in all the manners of blocking, on the spot, advancing and retreating.

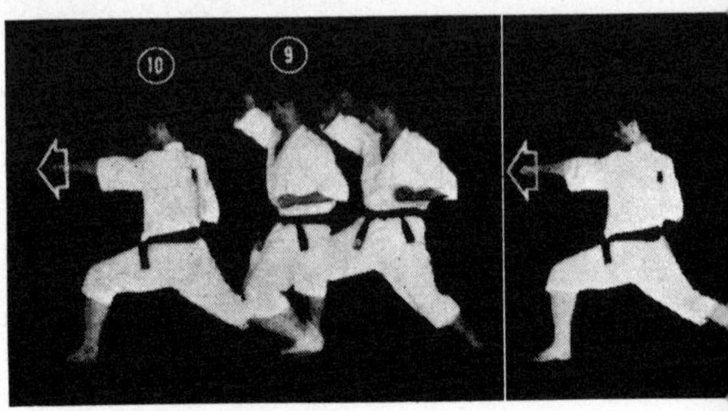

114

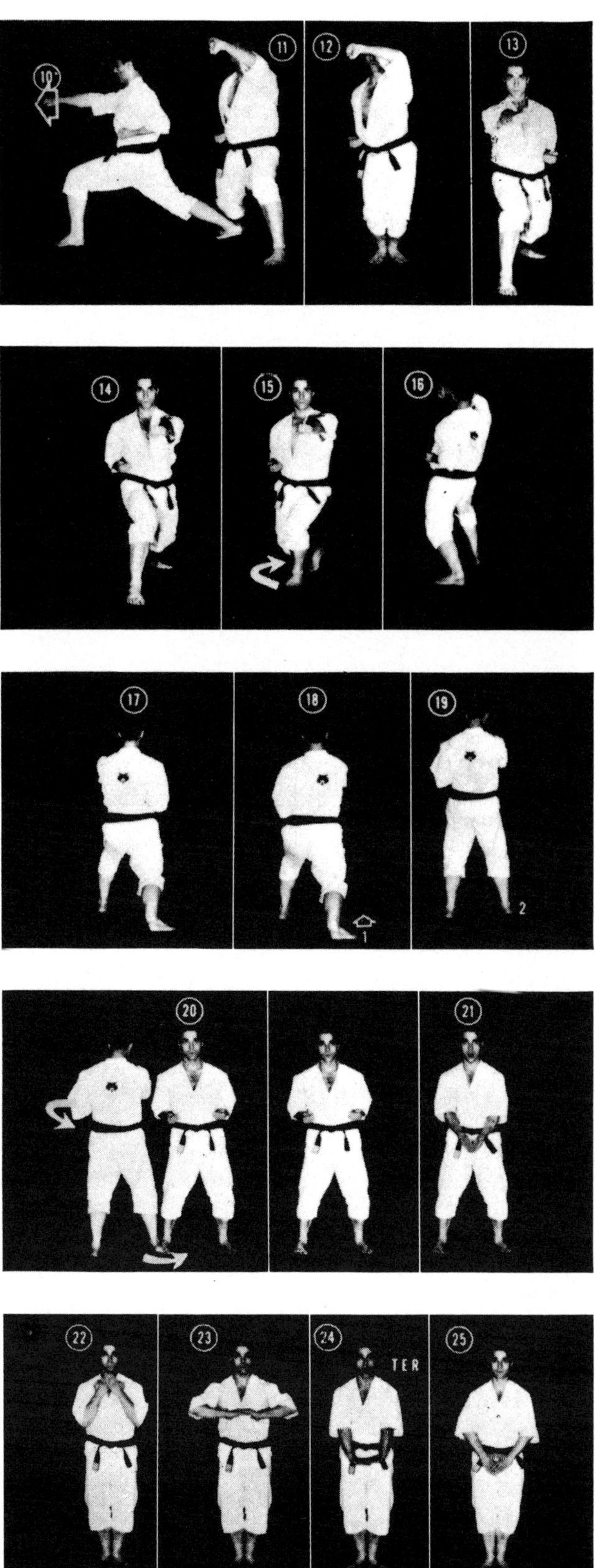
TER

Some Valuable Advice

This manual is for beginners. Accordingly, I shall give you here, in no particular order, some advanced advice which will be a veritable mine of "secrets" for those who read them. You may understand them at first glance, but as you progress, you will understand them better and often in a different way.

—There must always be an adversary present in spirit; at no time take your eyes off him, show your teeth or laugh.

—The spirit must draw together the body and the instincts.

—When the mind is dissipated, the physical and mental force which is in you loses its co-ordination.

—Painful exercises improve the concentration, and enable you to discover the truth about yourself.

—In every attack there is a problem of reaction, the force recoils on the attacker and he loses if his posture is defective (buttocks stuck out, shoulder moved back, heel raised or an incomplete Hikite), this also explains the unity of the direction of force. Execute everything in one solid, unified action, instantaneously.

—Mental concentration can lead to an apparent increase in weight, as well as efficacy.

—The eyes must attack first of all, followed by the foot then the fist, but all must reach the target at the same time.

—The important thing about an attack is . . . to strike.

—Unity of action takes precedence over the speed of the action.

—In order to be fast and supple at middle level, it is necessary to train very deep and low.

—Never at any moment lose your stability, for your opponent will not let it pass in real combat.

—Consider every Kata which you execute as a matter of life or death.

—Always try to really K.O. your partner in Gohon, Sanbon and Ippon-Kumite. This is your only chance to progress.

—In blocking, it is necessary to increase your own stability while making your adversary lose his. If he is better balanced or stronger than you are, you must unbalance him as you block.

—In every action, you must be aware of your own weak points (so as to defend them) and those of your opponent (so as to counter).

—It is necessary to rediscover childlike purity and add to it the strength and speed of a man.

—Nobody has a Mastery of Karate, for it is the total mastery of body and spirit which is the aim of Karate. It is necessary then to pursue your training in order to approach the maximum.

—Before passing on to other types of counter-attack, master the Gyaku-tsuki shudan (middle level). But keep the others in mind.

116

—Put the finishing touches to your blocks, postures and attacks. The majority of 2nd and 3rd Dan black belts go back again to the beginner's Karate simply because it is quicker and stronger. The ultimate object is different. If not, you will be unable to extend your technique to cover the whole field of Karate.

—All the postures other than Zen-Kutsu, Ko-Kutsu or Kiba-Dachi are variations of these. The three basic postures should, ideally, have the same distance between feet and the same narrow spaces between the arms and the body, with differing distributions of weight.

—Everything which causes the shoulders to move forward is weak.

—Everything which is on the axis of your body (which is also the line on which is found the three or four vital points) is strong.

—Connected with the respiration, the body traverses successive periods of weakness and strength.

—The sides under your arms are very weak, to protect them always will also strengthen them.

—Perform Tsuki with your lower abdomen and your buttocks.

—Your force should go right through your opponent, not stop at his body.

—Do not curl up your toes and put strength into the ankles.

—One cannot attack in Kokutsu without a period of "dead" time.

—It is the forward knee which "pulls" the body.

—Never put force in your shoulders, but under them.

—In attack and defence, think of the rotation of the wrist, for a small force can turn aside a great one.

—It is necessary to be always ready to block in all directions, to envelop yourself in a sensation of defence.

—In combat, your breathing should not be visible to your adversary.

—Karate can not be understood just by looking at it, but by work from the inside. It is not an intellectual game.

—Always keep the lips low, at the same level.

—The thumb must envelope the other clenched fingers, the little finger, being the weakest, should be folded first.

—Between block and counter-attack, the fist should remain firm, with gradations of the concentration of force invisible to the adversary.

—That which is essential is not the quantity or the beauty but the quality.

—It is necessary that those whom you meet to train you are not merely pleased to see you, but have respect for your efforts and intentions.

—It is the body and not the head which should remember the order and the development of a Kata.

—One should not stop breathing during a Kata, a Kumite or an attack, neither at the impact nor even afterwards.

—Try to find which is the strongest Oie-Tsuki or Gyaku-Tsuki.

—The power of the Hikite (withdrawing the arm to the side) should be greater than the attack or the block. Should the forearm be horizontal, downwards or upwards?

—The Kiai, an element of respiration, is just a consequence of the union of moral, psychical and physical force at its culminating point.

—An effective action is always apparently simple, without particular force. A due amount of force should be employed in Kime.

—One blocks with the body, the arms are accessories.

—Is the force of a Tsuki at middle level rising, descending or horizontal? Is its maximum efficacy the same?

—When making several attacks in pursuit (in the middle of Eian Shodan, for example), your buttocks when viewed from the back should not appear to move.

—It is not a good thing to think of nothing but Karate, to make it an obsession, it is better to train everyday with sincerity and develop your other faculties for the rest of the time . . . for this is also part of Karate.

—The three elements of good Karate are speed—power—endurance.

—In each Kata, each Kihon and each Kumite, it is necessary to try and discover something and to have the impression that one has found more than in the last training.

—Kime is the penetration of the wave of Ki, or vital source of the body, in both attacking and blocking. Without Ki, without Kime, there is no true Karate.

LEXICON OF TECHNICAL TERMS
KARATE

AGETSUKI: rising blow with the fist.
AGE-UKE: rising block.
ASHIGATANA: side of the foot.
ASHIKUBI: ankle.
ASHI-NO-KO: coming in.
ASHI-NO-TACHI-KATA: ways of placing the feet.
ASHIURA: sole of the foot.
ASHIWAZA: foot techniques.
ASHIZOKO: instep.
ATEMIWAZA or ATEWAZA: methods of attacking vital points of the body.

BASAMI: (HASAMI): scissors.
BARAI (HARAI): sweep.
BU: combat.
BUJIN: warrior.

CHOKUTSURI: direct blow with the fist.
CH'UAN FA: Chinese School of a technique similar to Karate ("the way of the fist").
CHUDAN: middle level.
CHUDAN-TEGATANA-UKE: middle level defence with the edge of the hand.
CHUDANTSUKI: middle level attack with the fist.
CHUDAN-UKE: middle level defence.

DAKITE: hand hooked.
DAN: step, grade (black belt).
  Shodan: 1st Dan.
  Nidan: 2nd Dan.
  Sandan: 3rd Dan.
  Yodan: 4th Dan.
  Godan: 5th Dan.
  Rokudan: 6th Dan.
  Shichidan: 7th Dan.
  Hachidan: 8th Dan.
  Kudan: 9th Dan.
  Judan: 10th Dan.
  Juichidan: 11th Dan
  Juni Dan: 12th Dan.
  Shihan: a Master.

EMPI: elbow (in Samuri language).
EMPI-UCHI: elbow inside (see uchi).
ENGISEN: line of demonstration.

FUDOTACHI: immobile posture.
FUDO-NO-SHISEI: immobile posture with heels together in Wado-Ryu.
FUKUSHIKI KUMITE: double assault or combat Kata.
FUKUSHIN: assistant judge.
FUMIKIRI: step out.
FUMIKOMI: crushing the foot.
FUMITSUKI: stamping down.
FUSEGI: defence.
FUSEN-CHO: victory by default.

GAKU: written diploma.
GAMAN KAMAE: waiting posture.
GEDAN: low level.
GEDAN KAMAE: low guard.
GEDAN-BARAI: low block (sweeping).
GEDANTSUKI: low attack.
GEDAN-UKE: low block (blocking).
GEIKO (KEIKO): training, practice.
GEKKEN: Japanese fencing.
GEKKENKA: fencer.
GERI (KERI): kick.
GETA: clogs of wood or metal (Karate).
GOHON-KUMITE: assault of five attacks and five paces.
GONIN-NUKI: combat continued for five successive attacks for one point.
GONIN-GAKE: one against five.
GO-NO-SEN: taking the initiative while the opponent is attacking, counter-attack
GOREI: order.
GYAKU: opposing or contrary action.
GYAKU-ZUKI: blow with the fist inversely to the feet.

HA: edge of the blade.
HABAKI-MOTO: thick part of the blade.
HACHI-MAKI-head bandage.
HACHI-JITACHI: waiting posture.
HAISHU: back of the hand.
HAISOKU: instep.
HAITO: internal edge of the hand (thumb side).
HAJIME: begin, commence, "Go" (referee's call).
HAKAMA: traditional skirt-type garment
HANEAGE: lifting the blade after lowering that of the opponent
HANGETSU-DACHI: wide sanchin posture.
HANSHI: higher rank as Kendo Master (at least 7th Dan).
HANSHIN: combat guard with one hand in Kendo.
HARAI: beaten (Kendo)—sweeping (Judo and Karate).
HANMI: Wado Ryu posture with one leg slightly advanced.

120

HANMI-NO-NEKOASHI: a three-quarters nekoashi.
HANSOKU-MAKE!: beaten as a result of violation of the rules.
HANTEI: decision; referee's call when demanding the decision of the vice-referees (arm raised vertically).
HARAI: see Barai (B in a composite word. H at the start of a composite word).
HARAITE: sweeping with the hand.
HASEN-KATA: wave; Kata in the form of a wave.
HASSO-KAMAE: guard with the sword held near the right shoulder.
HEI!: one of the Kiai sounds.
HEISOKU-TACHI: posture with the feet together.
HEN: phase, section.
HENKA: variant of the basic style.
HIDARI: left.
HIHO: secret method.
HIJI: elbow.
HIJIATE: attack with the elbow.
HIKIAGE: zanshin movement in a high posture after having struck.
HIKI-DO: striking the side while withdrawing.
HIKI-MEN: striking to the head while withdrawing.
HIKITE: pulling the hand back to the rear.
HIKIWAKE: draw (arm horizontal)
HINERITE: torsion of the hand.
HINERI-YOKO-EMPI: torsion of the elbow to the rear.
HIRA-HASAMI: flat scissors.
HIRAKEN-ZUKI: in Tsuki (direct) with the first two phalanges of the fist.
HIRIKI ASHI: side, pivot, step.
HIZA (or HITTSUI): knee (HITTSUI in Samuri language).
HITTSUI-GERI: blow with the knee.
HIZAGASHIRA: kneecap.
HIZAMAZUKU: kneeling (Kendo salute).
HIZA-TSUKI: on the knees.
HIZATSUI: the knee used to strike.
HODOKU: separate the blades.
HON: fundamental.

IAI: the art of unsheathing the sword before the combat commences; in Karate, the art of attacking while the opponent is deciding to go on the offensive.
IPPON: one (referee's call when a point is scored).
IPPON-KEN: fist with just the index finger folded.
IPPON-KUMITE: conventional assault with one attack.
IPPON-NUKITE: tip of the index finger.

JIKAN: limit of the contest period ("Time").
JITSU: technique, art—means also "true" (attack)
JIYU-IPPON-KUMITE: assault, one attack.
JIYU-KUMITE: free assault without a referee
JODAN: high level.
JODAN-KAMAE: high guard.
JOSEKI: the place of honour.

JUBAN NO MA-AI: perfect combat distance.
JUJI-UKE: block with the arms crossed.
JUNBI-TAISHO (or JUNBI-UNDO): suppling and warming exercises.
JUN-TSUKI: as Oie-Tsuki in Wado Ryu.
JUTSU: see JITSU.

KACHI-MAKE: combat to the finish, with no semi-victory.
KACHITE: absolute victor.
KAESHI: counter-attack, counter like a wave.
KAGI-ZUKI: hooked blow.
KAITE: instruction to turn.
KAKATO: heel.
KAKE-DAMESHI: test of strength (Kendo).
KAKETE: hand hooked.
KAKETEBIKI: training garments of Karate.
KAKE-UKE: hooked block.
KAKE-WAZA: hooking techniques.
KAKUTO: fist bent.
KAMAE: on guard.
KAMIZA (or JOZA): seat of honour.
KARATEKA (KARA: empty): specialist in Karate (KA: a person).
KANKU: Kata from which were taken parts of the EIAN and PINAN—there are two Kanku: DAI and SHO.
KATA: form. A collection of techniques performed in a pre-arranged way in order to mould the practitioner in a style. Also means "shoulder".
KATAKI: adversary.
KATANA: two-handed sword.
KATANA-KAKE: action of the sword.
KATANA NO HIRA: flat of the blade.
KATANA WO SASU: carry a sword.
KATATE-UCHI: one-handed blow with a sword.
KATSUGI: position of attack for the side
KEAGE: rising.
KEIKO: training.
KEGA: injury.
KEIKOBA: place of training.
KEIKOGI: training clothes (Judogi, Karategi, Kendogi, Aikidogi).
KEITO: base of the thumb; the wrist "cocked".
KEKOMI: penetrating (ex. Yokogeri-Kekomi).
KEMPO: ancient and primitive form of Karate.
KEN (i): general term for a sword—Also means a sword with two cutting edges (Tsurugi).
KENDO: Japanese fencing with a bamboo "sword" held in both hands.
KENJUTSU: the art of the real sword (or else Kendo).
KENKAKU: reputed fencer, a Master at Arms.
KENSEI: Kiai+concentration (can be silent).
KENSHUSEI: student selected for advanced studies
KEN WO FURU: to brandish a sword.
KAWASHI: dodge, parry.
KENTSUI: side of the fist.

KERIAGE: rising kick.
KERIGAESHI: a kick in return.
KERIKOMI: enter with a kick.
KERIWAZA: kicking techniques.
KI-AI: can be silent or audible (see Kensei).
KIBADACHI: horseback posture.
KIHON KUMITE: study training.
KIME: penetrating efficacy.
KIRI: cutting.
KIRITSU: standing.
KISSAKI: point of the sword.
KOBUSHI: normal fist.
KODACHI: small sword.
KODANSHA: black belt of 5th Dan or above.
KODOGU: sword furniture.
KO-EMPI: elbow to the rear.
KOGEKI: a sincere attack.
KOKO: "tiger's mouth" (index).
KOKORO-E: sincere spirit of comprehension.
KOKUTSUTACHI: posture with the weight on the rear leg.
KOSHI: "tiger's tooth". Ball of the foot.
KOTE: forearm, wrist.
KOTEN-SHIAI: individual competition.
KUMADE: "bear's paw" (palm with the fingers folded, used to attack the ears, jaw, etc.).
KUMITE: "meeting of the hands" = an assault.
KWAIKEN: small dagger carried in the clothing.
KYO: deception, a feint in combat.
KYO-JITSU: attack following a feint attack (the "one-two").
KYOSHI: grade of assistant professor.
KYU: class, lower grade (nine in Karate, six in Judo, Aikido and Kendo).
KYUSHO: vital points.

MA-AI (or MA): personal combat distance.
MACHI-DOJO: private dojo.
MAE: front, facing.
MAE-GERI: forward kick.
MAE-TOBI-KERI: jumping forward kick.
MAHANMI-NO-NEKOASHI: nekoashi posture sideways.
MAKE-KATA: the loser.
MAKETA: defeat.
MAKI-KOTE: variation.
MAKI-OTOSU: twisting to the ground.
MAKIWARA: padded post for striking practice.
MATO: vulnerable point.
MAWASHI-GERI: circular kick.
MAWASHI-ZUKI: circular blow with the fist.
MEN: Kendo mask or top of the head.
MEN-DARE: protective padding for the head and shoulders on a Kendo mask.
MEN-GANE: grill of a Kendo mask.

MEN-HIMO: cords of the mask.
MI: blade.
MI-ATERU: striking the body, "close quarters".
MIGI: right.
MIGI-MEN: vulnerable point on the right side of the top of the head.
MIKAZUKI-GERI: kick across the body.
MIKAZUKI-GERI-UKE: block with the foot across the body.
MIZU NO KOKORO: "the mind like water".
MON: escutcheon, armorial bearings.
MONO-UCHI: part of the blade.
MONTEI: disciple, student.
MOROTE-UCHI: blow with both fists.
MOROTE-UKE: block reinforced by the other hand (two hands: morote).
MOROTE-ZUKI: attack with both hands (separately or one reinforcing the other).
MUDANSHA: student of Kyu grade.
MUFUDAKAKE: tablet bearing the names of the seniors.
MUNE: back of the blade; the chest.

NAGASHI-UKE: sweeping block.
NAGEASHI: throw with the foot (Kendo, Karate).
NAGE-WAZA: throwing techniques.
NAGINATA: lance with a short blade.
NAIFU-ANCHI-TACHI: posture "against a knife".
NAKADATE-IPPON-KEN: fist with a knuckle extended.
NAKAYUBI-IPPONKEN: fist with the middle knuckle extended.
NAKAYUWAI: striking part of the shinai.
NAMIGAESHI: defence in wave form.
NAYASHI: to press the opposing blade against the ground while trying for a point
NEKO-ASHI-TACHI: posture of a cat.
NIDAN-KERI: kick at two levels.
NIHON KATANA: combat with two swords (one in each hand).
NIHON ME: the "decider" in combat.
NIHON-NUKITE: tips of the index and middle fingers.
NIHON-SHOBU: match of two points.
NI-TO: two swords.
NOBASU: to stretch, extend.
NUKI-AWASERU: to engage.
NUKI-DO: parry an attack and strike at the side at the same time.
NUKITE: finger-tips.
NUKI-TSUKE: cut with the sword as in iai.
NUKI-UCHI: strike and cut in the same movement

OBI: belt.
OIETSUKI: attack in pursuit.
OJIGI: ceremonial salute (Kendo)
OJI-KAESHI: parry—riposte.
OKINAWA-TE: Karate of Okinawa.
OMOTE: upper part.

124

OSAERU: to hold.
OSAE-UKE: maintained block (pushing).
OTOSHI: to push the opposing blade strongly downwards.

PINAN (EIAN): Eian in the Shotokan technique and Pinan in the others. There are five Katas.

REI: salute, etiquette.
REIGISAHO: rules of etiquette in the Dojo.
RENSHI: the lowest of the Kendo instructional grades (minimum 4th Dan).
RENZOKUTSUKI: successive attacks with the fist.
RIKEN (or URAKEN): back of the fist.
RITSUREI: traditional salute.
RYU: system, a method which has formed a school in Budo.
RYUGI: the style of a school or a Dojo.

SA!: interjection meaning, roughly, "let's go!"
SAGETA EMPI: the elbow in low position.
SAGI-ASHITACHI: posture of a heron.
SAKIGAWA: leather tip to the Shinai.
SAMURAI: Japanese warrior in the service of an overlord.
SANBON-KUMITE: assault of three attacks (generally three steps).
SANCHIN-DACHI: posture with the knees pulled in.
SANKAKUTOBI: triple, jumping blow (horizontal).
SAN-NEN-GOROSHI: secret method of delivering attacks which cause delayed death, such
    as "death in three years".
SANSENTACHI: posture of the three battles.
SASAE-UKE: a maintained defence.
SEIGAN: normal Kendo guard.
SEIKEN: normal fist.
SEIRYUTO: base of the outer edge of the hand.
SEIZA: posture of meditation similar to ZAZEN.
SEMETE: attacker in a Karate Kata.
SEN: initiative, positive.
SEN-NO-SEN: the highest form of initiative, taking the advantage just before the opponent's
    attack.
SENSEI: the leading professor of a Dojo.
SENKEN: anticipation.
SHASHIN: deliberate opening in combat.
SHI: warrior.
SHIAI: refereed contest, competition.
SHIAIJO: contest area.
SHICHIDAN-KERI-NO-RENSHUHO: training in seven kicks.
SHIHAN: Master of exceptional quality and very high grade.
SHINTAI: movement of the body.
SHIZENHONTAI: natural, basic posture.
SHOCHUGEIKO: special Summer training.

SHIHO-TSUKI-NO-KATA: Kata of four corners.
SHIKOTACHI: horseback posture with the feet turned outwards (Sumo posture).
SHIMOSEKI: lower side.
SHIMOZA: lower seat.
SHIMPAN: judgement.
SHIMEI: attack with deadly possibilities (for "Ippon" in Karate).
SHINAI: split bamboo sword used in Kendo.
SHINKO-KATA: advanced Kata.
SHINKYU-SHIAI: promotion competition for Kyu grades.
SHIRIZOKU: to withdraw oneself.
SHI-TACHI: in Kendo, the counter-attacker in a Kata.
SHIWARI (or TAME-SHIWARI): breaking tests.
SHIZENTAI: natural posture.
SHOBU: official contest.
SHODAN: lowest of the Dan grades (1st Dan).
SHUGEKI: Kendo attack.
SHUSHIN: judge or principal referee.
SHUTO: edge of the hand.
SHUTO-UCHI: direct attack with the edge of the hand.
SHUTO-UKE: defence with the edge of the hand reversed.
SOCHIN-DACHI: a posture similar to Zen Kutsu but wider, and the advanced foot is more
    turned.
SOKUTO: edge of the foot.
SORASHI: false attack.
SOTO: exterior, (principally the exterior of the opponent).
SOTO-UKE: exterior block, for the most part with Tetsui (side of the fist) or Uchi-Komi
(according to the position).
SUBURI: free exercise with the sword.
SUKI: opening.
SUSUMU: to advance.
SUWARI: to sit down.

TACHI: ceremonial sword hung from the belt.
TACHIKAKI: old term for Kenjutsu.
TAI: body, also used in describing posture.
TAIKO: face-to-face, opposed.
TAIKYOKU-NO-KATA: Kata for developing the body (there are six Taikyoku).
TAITO: sword carrier.
TAKE: bamboo.
TANSHIKI KUMITE: simple Kumite.
TANTO: dagger.
TATE-EMPI: the elbow used vertically.
TATE-ZUKI: vertical blow with the fist.
TATSU: standing.
TATSUJIN: fencing expert (in the sense of someone who is hard to bring down).
TE: hand.
TEGATANA: edge of the hand (with the idea of using the edge of the hand like a sword).
TE-HANARE: one hand on the sword.

TEISHO: base of the palm.
TEISOKU: instep.
TEKUBI: wrist.
TEKKI-NO-KATA: the "iron horseman" Kata. There are three Tekki Katas.
TEMOTO: strong part of the blade.
TENUGUI: small handkerchief carried in the belt in Kendo.
TEN-NO-KATA: "Heavenly Kata", executed alone or with a partner.
TETTSUI: side of the fist (the "iron hammer").
TEWAZA: hand techniques.
TO: sword.
TOBI-KOMI: to jump in.
TOBIGOSHI: to jump outside (not the same as in Judo).
TOBIGERI: a jumping kick.
TOBIKOMIASHI: to jump into the legs.
TOBIKOMI-TSUKI: blow with the fist while jumping (in Wado Ryu, while taking a big step
    forward).
TOI: out of range.
TOKUI-TSUKI: favourite technique (the "pet" blow with the fist).
TO-JIN-HO: method of falling, different to the Judo Ukemi which needs a tatami.
TSUBA: sword guard.
TSUBAZERIAI: the sword guards touching.
TSUGI-ASHI: moving with one foot following the other without crossing. (normal: AYUMI
    ASHI).
TSUKA: gripping the sword.
TSUKAGAWA: rolling-up the Shinai.
TSUKAMI-UKE: block with a grip.
TSUKERU: attack, taking.
TSUKI (or ZUKI): direct attack as if plunging in a knife; in Kendo, a thrust with the point
    of the sword to the throat; in Karate, a direct attack with the fist.
TSUKI-DARE: throat protector on a Kendo mask.
TSUKI NO KOKORO: spirit like the moon.
TSUKITE: the hand performing Tsuki.
TSUKI-UKE: stopping blow.
TSUKI-WAZA: technique of direct blows.
TSUKOMI: blow with the fist with the upper part of the body inclined forwards (gyakutsuki
    in Jun-Tsuki).

UCHI: attack. In Karate, it generally signifies the exterior towards the interior, or from an
    upper to a lower position, through opposition to the reverse.
UCHITSUKI-BU: the most effective part of the blade for cutting.
UCHI-MAJIRI: free-for-all (combat).
UCHI-MAKE: a scoring cut in Kendo.
UCHI-TACHI: the attacker in Kendo Kata.
UCHI-UKE: internal defence.
UDE: arm, forearm.
UDE-UKE: block with the forearm
UE-NI: on the head.
UKE: defence.

UKE-DACHI: to stop an attack with the sword (Kendo).
UKE-KAESHI: parry and riposte.
UKE-KOTAE: riposte.
UKETE: defence with the hand (Karate Kata).
URA: back, non-cutting edge of the sword.
URAKEN: back of the fist.
URA-ZUKI: blow with the fist at close range.
USHIRO: the rear, the back.
USHIRO-GERI: backward kick.

WAKI-KAMAE: side guard.
WAKIZASHI: the shortest of a pair of swords.
WAZA: technique (ex. TE-WAZA).
WATSUKI: circular blow with the fist.

YABURI (DOJO YABURI): literally "break the house down", to defy a Dojo.
YAKUSOKU-KUMITE: conventional Kumite.
YAMA-ZUKI: "mountain punch" (in an upwards direction).
YAME!: in Karate: return to the starting position. "Stop!" in Kendo.
YARI: lance.
YARIDO: fencing with the lance.
YASUME: rest, relax.
YOI: instruction to get prepared.
YOKERU: lateral evasion.
YOKO: side.
YOKO-GERI: kick to the side.
YOKO-TOBI-GERI: jumping kick to the side.
YONHON-NUKITE: points of the four fingers together.
YORIASHI: approach.
YUBI-HASAMI: scissor with the fingers.
YUDANSHA: black belt holder.
YUMI-KOBUSHI: wrist flexed.
YUMI-UKE: bent defence.

ZANSHIN: a state of alertness after having struck or before.
ZAZEN: a sitting posture for mental concentration.
ZEN: Japanese interpretation of Buddhism.
ZEN-EMPI: frontal blow with the elbow.
ZENGO-EMPI: blow with the elbow to the front and back.
ZEMPO-UKEMI: method of breaking a forward fall.
ZENKUTSU-DACHI: posture with the forward leg flexed.
ZUKI (or TSUKI): see TSUKI. Pronounced ZUKI in a word and TSUKI at the beginning,
    but always written TSUKI.